MW01702995

Dare To Be Queen

A Wholistic & Comprehensive Curriculum for Girls

Urban Leadership Institute

HOTEP PRESS

ISBN 0-9659028-7-0

For information address: Hotep Press, 2437 Maryland Avenue, Baltimore, Maryland 21218

The Dare to Be Queen Curriculum is dedicated to
Kaalisha Ajala
Monique Armstrong
Jua Brooks
Kofi Brooks
Tasha Brown
Kelsye Miller
Mikalei Miller
Danyell Pritchett
Hadiya Shields
Sameera Shields
Alexis Smith
Tasha Suggs;
also to the memory of
Kena Crandel and Dain Mischa Duffie

CONTENTS

INTRODUCTION

Dare to Be Queen! Why a ***"Queen"***? The word ***"Queen"*** is an Old English term (*cwēn*) that dates as far back to the 11th Century and means "wife of a king." This term was derived from the Germanic word *kwēn-iz* which means "woman, wife, queen." The Germanic root for the word, *kwen-,* "woman," comes by Grimm's Law from the Indo-European root *g^{w}en-,* "woman," which appears in at least two other English words borrowed from elsewhere in the Indo-European family. One is *gynecology,* from Greek *gunē,* "woman." Another, less obvious one is *banshee,* "woman of the fairies," the wailing female spirit attendant on a death, from Old Irish *ben,* "woman."

History gives us to know that there were and are still many, many queens. There was Queen Rikissa, Queen Ingamodher and Queen Ingegard Haradsdotter—all from Sweden. There was Queen Elizabeth I and Mary Queen of Scots. These two queens are recorded as having a very complicated and deadly relationship. Many of us are perhaps more familiar with Queen Elizabeth I, wife of King Henry VIII, who is also known as the "Genius of the Golden Age." There were also the Great Queens of Africa: Nzignha, Queen of Matamba; Nefertiti, Nubian Queen of Egypt, Cleopatra VII, Queen of Egypt; Yaa Asantewa, Queen of Ghana; and Nandi, Queen of Zululand.

Since its initial inception, the word ***"Queen"*** has taken on as many as six different meanings to date. For the sake of the Dare to Be Queen Curriculum, however, we will speak from the American Heritage Dictionary of the English Language, Fourth Edition's fourth definition. This particular definition states that a ***"Queen"*** is something personified as a woman who is considered the best or most important of her kind.

Inasmuch as we are well aware that middle and high school girls are not yet women, our goal is that this curriculum will serve as the catalyst with which we educate and empower girls to become woman who are indeed considered the best or most important of their kind. By exposing girls to relevant and applicable activities as well as having them engage in honest, cleansing group dialogue guided by a responsible adult, we believe there is great potential to address and bring resolution to some of the dynamics girls are dealing with every day. We further believe that by teaching girls in their primal years the power of constructively confronting and resolving issues—on all levels—we instill in them a practice that will hopefully govern them for the rest of their lives.

In Dare to Be Queen, we parallel the process of becoming a queen with that of being a "Five Star Girl," hence the illustration of the five stars on each page. As many of us are aware "Five Star" represents the best…top of the line…head of the class…cream of the crop. Dare to Be Queen is indeed a curriculum that employs girls to aspire to reach a level of being that is indicative of their fullest potential and their greatest good. The Five Star Girl Pledge, which is located on page 7 is an affirming mantra we hope girls will commit to memory and allow to become a part of their daily ritual for the rest of their lives.

The American Heritage® Dictionary of the English Language, Fourth Edition
Copyright © 2000 by Houghton Mifflin Company.
Published by Houghton Mifflin Company.

Message to Youth Development Practitioners

The **Urban Leadership Institute** is pleased that you have purchased the *Dare to Be Queen* Curriculum. The curriculum is designed to engage adolescent females around issues related to personal development, womanhood and value clarification. With the alarming rates of delinquency and violence among girls, the curriculum provides professionals with a "blue print" to engage girls in a variety of subject matters.

The curriculum focuses on primary prevention through addressing self-esteem, self-awareness and decision making among teen girls ages 12-17. The curriculum is based on numerous focus groups with girls across the country along with interviews of professionals who have a track record of working with adolescent girls. The curriculum features twelve modules, a host of developmental activities, and a resource section developed to assist agencies with documenting program successes.

Finally, we feel that the *Dare to Be Queen* curriculum provides professionals with a solid instrument designed to engage adolescent girls around issues related to abstinence, media images and friendships.

We strongly encourage you to use the curriculum as well as attend one of our National Train-the-Trainer Certification Conferences. We would also like to take this opportunity to invite you to visit our web site www.urbanyouth.org for periodic updates of events and trainings.

David Miller, M.Ed.
Chief Visionary Officer
Urban Leadership Institute

MESSAGE TO PARTICIPANTS

Welcome to Dare to Be Queen! Welcome to a life-changing journey! Welcome to an experience you will not soon forget!

As a middle school or high school age girl it is very likely that you have already embarked upon experiences that have caused you to ask yourself questions like: *Should I or shouldn't I? Does he really care or is he just playin' me? Am I really too fat or too skinny? Is she really my friend or is she around for convenience? Why does my body feel this way? How could I possibly think that when I know better? Am I good enough? Why do I keep making the same dumb mistakes? Do my parents even care? Why does it seem like nobody understands me?*

To your surprise and our delight, we have strategically and sensitively designed this Dare to Be Queen Curriculum to help you with the complex aspects of your life you may need guidance in. Building a "Five Star Girl" who can take on the world is our mission and our intention. Hence, we are most confident in the content of Dare to Be Queen, and believe that you will have no other choice *but to be better* as you avail yourself to all that this curriculum has to offer.

It is our hope, therefore, that you will take this experience seriously. We invite you to be real. We encourage you to be honest. We employ you to interact with and get to know your fellow participants, because as you will soon find out, you all have more in common than not. We strongly advise you to listen – attentively – to the instructions as they are given. And finally, we cannot emphasize enough how important it is for you to connect with your group leader (the adult in charge of organizing your activities) to ensure that you get the most out of your time in this program. Don't be afraid to pull your leader to the side and share that a particular activity is causing you to become emotional, and as a result you need to be excused or talked with privately. Don't hesitate to tell him/her when you don't understand a directive or you aren't getting the meaning of the activity. Remember, Dare to Be Queen is for you and about you. If you miss its meaning you've missed an opportunity to enrich your life.

Your life—and your ability to life productively, abundantly, and successfully is what being a Five Star Girl is all about. No longer is it okay for you to haphazardly wonder through your days contemplating who you are; second guessing your potential; compromising your values; masking your pain while allowing others to call you out of your name. You are who the Creator created you to be and everything you need is within your ability to see. You must simply present yourself ready to receive and great things will begin to appear as you believe.

Mischa P. Green
Female Projects Coordinator
Urban Leadership Institute

PARENTS, TEACHERS & YOUTH LISTEN UP!

The girls in our lives are receiving a constant bombardment of destructive messages about their bodies. Media images teach them (and us) that their appearance is the most important thing about them, and that their appearance is never good enough. Because of these messages, girls are concentrating more on their looks than on their real life accomplishments. And in the effort to achieve the emaciated look which they are being trained to admire, girls are doing themselves real harm, physically and emotionally.

The $40 billion a year weight loss industry emits a continual stream of high-profile images which misrepresent what an "average" size woman looks like. In fact, the models in the ads we see are much smaller than average girls and women, and girls who attempt to look like those models rather than themselves frequently become casualties of the eating disorder epidemic that is sweeping America. The thinner-is-better standard of beauty hurts us all. How? By distracting girls from focusing on their real accomplishments; by making girls despise their own uniquely and divinely diverse female bodies; by removing $40 billion a year from our wallets; and by putting women of different sizes against each other in the beauty competition, rather than them uniting against the forces which oppress them all.

Please don't let the weight loss industry and the physicians in its pay teach their values to our daughters, nieces, granddaughters, and all the girls in our lives. We have to take responsibility for all the messages we give to girls, through our behavior as well as our words. We are a potential source of sanity, accurate information (as opposed to corporate propaganda), and political analysis.

For that reason, Urban Leadership Institute (ULI) was inspired to write Dare To Be Queen (DTBQ), an interactive, hands on curriculum that involves middle and high school girls working together to address issues of low self esteem, promote responsible decisions and to advocate for positive images of girls by the media and major retailers. Through their participation in the program, the curriculum will strengthen their own personal self-esteem and body image while discovering that they have powerful voices which are able to effect social, political, and personal change. ULI believes in the power of Five Star Girls, because the program provides young women with the tools, confidence, and self-esteem they need to impact one of the major influences in their lives—the media—on one of the most pressing teen health issues--body image. Research reveals that 40-60% of girls in high school perceive themselves to be overweight and are actively trying to lose weight. Approximately 10-15% of these girls can be considered "chronic dieters," two-thirds of whom are not overweight at all.

A nationwide poll of students ages 9-15, *Shortchanging Girls, Shortchanging America* (1991) examines the impact of gender on self-esteem, career aspirations, educational experiences, and interest in math and science. The study found that as girls reach adolescence, they experience a significantly greater drop in self-esteem than boys' experience. The poll also confirms a growing body of research that indicates girls are systematically, if unintentionally, discouraged from a wide range of academic pursuits--particularly in math and science. This gap in self-esteem and drop in girls' interest in math and science have devastating consequences for the future of girls and the future of the nation.

Unfortunately, poor body image is not simply a state of mind. In a country where at least 5-10 million women and girls have active, destructive eating disorders, including anorexia, bulimia, and binge eating disorder, dissatisfaction with one's size and shape too often has dire health consequences. Eating disorders are serious health conditions with one of the highest death rates of any mental illness. The emotional, physical, and financial destruction of eating disorders, however, need not occur. Eating disorders can be prevented and destructive behaviors corrected, and we believe the DTBQ program is one of the first steps in this process.

Through facilitated discussions, students in the program explore their own body image issues, general principles about eating healthy foods and thinking healthy thoughts, and the connection between media and body image. The Five Star Girls team members take an in-depth look at how advertisements are developed, and, in the process, gain an ability to analyze their underlying messages.

LaMarr Darnell Shields, M.Ed.
President
Urban Leadership Institute

FACILITATOR'S GUIDE TO USING THE MODULES EFFECTIVELY

Dare to Be Queen is deliberately designed with simplicity in mind. Though wholistic and comprehensive, Dare to Be Queen is purposely not complicated to implement. Because we understand that in many instances facilitators may not be in a position to spend a great deal of preparatory time, we have given step-by-step straight forward directives for each activity. As you become familiar with the curriculum you will notice a consistent sequential pattern throughout. The pattern consists of:

The Titled Module
Goals
Overview
Activity Titles
Fact Findings

There are 12 modules. These modules represent what our research suggests are some of the most profound areas of contention and/or threat for girls. It is therefore extremely important that facilitators make it their business to become familiar with the modules' principle theme as this theme is what guides every activity within that particular module.

Following the actual modules are two to four corresponding activities. The outline for each activity consists of:

The Activity Title
Purpose
Directions
Instructional Procedures
Materials Needed

All of the activities are middle and high school age appropriate, and are tactically crafted to stir up engaging dialogue, enhance educational interest, foster mental growth, stimulate spiritual awareness, and initiate psychological healing. Because some of the activities are such that they could potentially invoke an emotional response, we strongly suggest that facilitators are equipped to handle such occurrences.

As the facilitator, your role is critical. You represent the difference in girls getting this material or not. You are responsible for initiating the dialogue that introduces the modules as well as the activities. You, therefore, must be well versed on the various themes/topics covered in the modules.

FACILITATOR'S GUIDE TO USING THE MODULES EFFECTIVELY

Inasmuch as we have done our best to design Dare to Be Queen in such a way that the facilitator is not having to figure out what to do next, it is incumbent upon you, as the facilitator, to take the necessary time – prior to introducing a module or implementing an activity – to read thoroughly. Attempting to present this material without a clear understanding of its purpose unquestionably jeopardizes the effectively of the activities. As a result, participants are shortchanged and the experience of Dare to Be Queen is not as enriching and life-impacting as it is designed to be.

Within the activities you will notice different cue visuals. These cue visuals represent the key materials to be used in the activity:

Participants' Handout

Facilitator's Handout

A song

A movie/documentary

As illustrated in the cue visuals, many of the activities have handouts. Participant handouts are to be copied and distributed to each participant where the activity indicates. Facilitator's handouts are to be used by the facilitator *only* and are not to be distributed to the participants. Where a song is indicated, the lyrics of the song can be found in the back of the curriculum preceding the Appendix. Additionally, please be advised that the sessions which include viewing a movie/documentary will, in all probability, have to be covered over two sessions as the movie/documentary have running times of at least 80 – 90 minutes each.

In our efforts to ensure that Dare to Be Queen is in fact wholistic in nature, we designed a curriculum that we feel appeals to girls from different backgrounds with different experiences. The use of handouts, songs, movies and documentaries is indicative of an approach that is as diverse as the girls we seek to help. We, therefore, cannot stress enough how necessary it is for you to include into each activity everything that is a part of the activity. Read ahead to get a sense of what you'll need next and plan early—as far in advance as possible.

Please, please, please be mindful that as the facilitator you are to be as much involved in the activities as the participants. You must mirror the activities for the girls. If necessary, do the activity during your preparation time so that you have a sense of what to say and what to do. Make yourself a part of the activities. You cannot be a spectator, you must be a participator. Be willing, to the extent it's appropriate, to share some of your experiences. You might find that in some instances you have to take the lead until the girls become comfortable enough to follow. Your lead demonstrates that it's safe to talk…to be honest…to be real. Please do not underestimate the significance of your presence, nor the message that your openness conveys to the girls who are watching you.

FIVE STAR GIRL PLEDGE

The "Five Star Girl Pledge" represents a lifelong commitment each girl makes with herself. It is hoped that the five elements of this pledge will serve as five anchors that essentially keeps each girl safely put in the truth of who she is. The overall purpose of the pledge is to be carefully explained prior to engaging in the modules. Each element is to be thoroughly broken down and elaborated upon so that every girl fully understands the significance of what she is reciting.

The Five Star Girl Pledge is to be recited at the opening and closing of each group session with the participants in a circle holding hands. The significance of the circle is that it symbolizes unity and collectivity. The clasping of hands symbolizes the bond that is formed every time a girl grabs hold of another girls' hand. Finally, the circle stores the energy of everyone in it, and allows each person to be blessed and helped by others within the circle.

☆ I am the best—not because of what others think, but because of what I know.

☆ I am abundantly rich in ability. There is nothing I cannot be.

☆ I am a unique display of authentic beauty—not because of physical appearance but because of the content of my heart and the wholesomeness of my thought.

☆ I am mindful of my imperfections that will neither handicap nor imprison me as long as I keep a healthy perspective about what I see.

☆ I am my sister's friend. I need her and she needs me; Five Star Girls understand the power and the strength of *we.*

GETTING STARTED

It was once said, "You cannot teach a people you do not believe in." Strangely enough, many persons attempt to teach other people they have very little or no belief in. Daily, persons superficially embark upon imparting understanding to others while doubting, all the while, these individuals' capacity to grasp that which is being imparted. Well, there are no two ways about it; to effectively implement Dare to Be Queen one must unequivocally believe in girls. One must believe in their limitless potential. One must believe in their capacity to change. One must believe in their ability to persevere. One must understand the gender called female and be openly willing to learn as you teach, get as you give, and share as it is appropriate.

In addition to believing in girls, you must be cognizant of their issues, their distractions, as well as their uniqueness. Talk to them. Listen to them. Get in their space. Hear their stories. Watch their signals. Learn their language. All of these things will help you to better help them.

Once you are fully confident of your belief in girls and your commitment to wanting to be a part of their development, you can move forward in the Dare to Be Queen curriculum. Initially it would serve you well to become familiar with the entire curriculum by reading it through and through—understanding that everything on every page has its purpose. As you read through the curriculum pay close attention to the messages of the authors. These messages will give you a peep into the minds of the authors who felt Dare to Be Queen was necessary. Don't skip over the Introduction for it declares the value and the purpose of this instrument. Because each one of us has a role to play in our girls' development, the Message to Parents/Caregivers is something you absolutely want to share with the parents/caregivers of your participants. It is one thing for the parents/caregivers to enroll their children, but it's another thing for them to involve themselves in their child's developmental process.

The modules, as you may know, are the crux of the curriculum. It stands to reason that you must read the Facilitator's Guide to Using the Modules Effectively as this tells you how to maneuver through the modules and their corresponding activities. The modules immediately follow the guide to using the modules. Again, as the facilitator you must become thoroughly familiar with the modules. As you prepare to implement the activities within the modules, remember to use your Session Checklist and Session Attendance Sheet, which are the first two pages in the Appendix. These forms will help to keep you organized. Leave nothing to chance. You can best implement Dare to Be Queen *after* you have gotten to know the curriculum.

Use plenty of tabs or post-its to indicate the pages you need to copy. Whether a handout for an activity or a form for the participant and/or her parents/caregivers; know where your forms are and at what point you are to use them. The Appendix, for example, is the primary place for all of the forms. Go through the Appendix to learn what forms are there. Get familiar with your record keeping paperwork like the Youth Consent Form, the Youth Contract and the Parent Contract. The bottom line, organization is key to a successful implementation.

CURRICULUM MODULES & ACTIVITIES OUTLINE

Module One: Who Am I &Why Am I Here
- Setting a Solid Foundation
- Maximizing the Moment
- A Busy Life for Kids

Module Two: Values & Virtue
- Building a Secure Me
- Throne Life
- Final Hour
- This I Know . . .

Module Three: My Body . . . My Business
- Campaign for the Cause
- You Are What You Eat
- Real Women Have Curves

Module Four: Sealing the Sacred
- Role Play: You Should Have Known Better
- Stairway to Love & Respect – Without Sex
- Straight Talkin' Roundtable

Module Five: A Scholar I Am
- Lobbying to Learn . . . Learning to Lobby
- Urban Leadership Excursion
- Criss Cross Word Toss

Module Six: Anger Management 101
- Girlhood
- Managing Me

CURRICULUM MODULES & ACTIVITIES OUTLINE

Module Seven: I Choose to Forgive
- Forgiveness & Me
- It's Never Too Late
- Poetically Speaking

Module Eight: Friendships & Relationships
- Treat Her Like a Lady
- The Measuring Stick of Friendship
- Healthy vs. Unhealthy Relationships

Module Nine: Family Dynamics
- Vignette: Who Do I Tell?
- Outsider
- Confession Is Good for the Soul

Module Ten: The Father Factor
- Self Esteem Autobiography
- Timeline
- Where Are the Fathers?

Module Eleven: Hip Hop's Affect on Girls
- A Journey Into Me
- Body Image/Self Identity

Module Twelve: Baggage Check
- Trash Can I Am Not
- Circle of Security
- Ladder of Success vs. Pile of Regrets

Module One:
Who Am I & Why Am I Here

Five Star Girl Quote:
"You must live within your sacred truth."
Hausa Proverb

Module Goals:

1. To set in place a healthy and concrete foundation of our reason for being.
2. To acquaint girls with the dangers associated with taking on too much too soon.

Module Overview:

As we go through life we will endeavor to become many things. We will have to operate in numerous capacities. We will be forced to handle many responsibilities—in many instances all at the same time. The challenge with doing so many things, having to be in so many places, and being needed by so many people is quite often we get so caught up in doing, getting, giving, and becoming that we forget who we are and/or fail to connect with the truth of why we are here.

Although this tends to happen more frequently in the lives of young adult and adult woman, the pressure and presence of such demands are quickly engulfing the lives of teen girls as well. There is the demand to excel academically coupled with being team captain. There is the demand to be a No. 1 daughter coupled with being a faithful best friend. There is the demand to keep up with the latest fashions coupled with a job to make certain you have the financial means to keep up with the latest fashions, and the list builds on. But before you allow yourself to get all caught up in the hype of a busy, potentially out of control existence it is important that you ground yourself in the knowledge of who you are and why you are here.

Before you buy into the compulsion to be who people say you ought to be. And before you make decisions that come with a lot of responsibility and pressure, it is important for you to know that you are a uniquely made, purposely planted creation of the Creator placed here to be about a great work. Hence, you must constantly examine what you are doing, why you are doing it, and how you are doing it to make certain that whatever you involve yourself in is a good reflection of who you are as well as compliments or gets you closer to where you want to go and who you want to ultimately be.

Module Activities:

1. Setting a Solid Foundation
2. Maximizing the Moment
3. A Busy Life for Kids

Fact Finding:

- **80% of middle and high school students take part in organized activities after school and on weekends, and most of these young people have something scheduled nearly every day.**
- **41% of parents want their child to be involved in organized activities outside of school hours to develop their interests and hobbies, while 27% want to keep their child busy and out of trouble.**

Source: Associated Press

Activity 1: Setting a Solid Foundation

Activity Purpose:

The purpose of this activity is to give girls an up-close and personal look at how important setting a foundation is, and how it impacts our ability to build quality lives.

Directions:

Each girl will be given 14 popsicle sticks, some craft glue, 5 pebbles, and a black permanent marker. The craft glue and markers can be shared amongst the girls. The girls are then instructed by way of a visual demonstration how to begin to glue their respective foundations together using the popsicle sticks and the craft glue. Once the foundations are together, the girls will then write on the pebbles five things that will be symbolic of what they would like their foundations to be made of.

Instructional Procedures:

1. Open with the "Five Star Girl Pledge".
2. Begin with a discussion about a solid foundation.
3. Introduce activity and give step by step directions.
4. Have each girl talk about what their foundation consists of and why.
5. Distribute "The Benefits of Having a Solid Foundation" handout.
6. Always end the activity with the "Five Star Girl Pledge".

Materials Needed:

1. Popsicle sticks
2. Craft glue
3. Pebble rocks
4. Permanent markers (black)

The Benefits of Having a Solid Foundation

Our foundation is the essence of who we are. Our foundation is what primarily defines us. Having a solid foundation is essential to everyone's well being as our foundation is that which grounds us, anchors us, and secures us. Below are five benefits of having a solid foundation.

- We know who we are, because our foundation dictates our place of belonging.
- We have an anchor that will not allow us to be lifted but so far up from where we belong.
- We have a point of reference in the event we lose our way.
- We have something in which to firmly plant our feet upon.
- We have something upon which to build from.

Module 1 Activity 1 Handout

ACTIVITY 2: Busy Bee. . .

Activity Purpose:

The purpose of this activity is to teach girls the importance of prioritizing at an early age so as to prevent the onset of the stress and anxiety that is common to being overwhelmed from taking on more than you actually feel like you can physically handle.

Directions:

The girls are instructed to list on the **Prioritizing** handout those things they see as priorities now—pre learning of prioritizing, which is referred to as the *Before*. The facilitator will then give a 10 minute lecture on prioritizing as well as demonstrate strategies on how to effectively prioritize. Following the lecture, the girls are instructed to flip the handout over and re-prioritize the list they initially wrote to reflect how they will prioritize in the future—post learning of prioritizing, which is referred to as the *After*. Once both sides have been completed, the girls will be instructed to examine the papers to see if there are any differences. The girls will then close the activity by talking about any challenges they may see with actually implementing the *After* process.

Instructional Procedures:

1. Open with reciting the Five Star Girl Pledge.
2. Begin with a discussion about prioritizing. What it means? Why it's important?
3. Have girls talk for a few minutes about women they may know who carry a heavy load and wear a lot of hats. Also, ask if they themselves have ever experienced any stress because they've taken on too much.
4. Introduce activity and give step by step directions.
5. Distribute the **Prioritizing** handout.
6. Encourage the girls who will to discuss their *Before* and *After* papers as well as any barriers to implementation of the *After* process.
7. Always end the activity with the Five Star Girl Pledge.

Materials Needed:

1. **Prioritizing** handout
2. Pens or pencils

Prioritizing

It is extremely easy, yet very dangerous to bite off more than one can chew. All too often we tell ourselves that we can handle more than we actually can. And by taking on more than we can handle, we cause ourselves and sometimes those around us a lot of unnecessary stress. The purpose of this activity is to take a look at and compare how you prioritize now versus how you prioritize after getting a better understanding of prioritizing.

BEFORE

1. ______________________________

2. ______________________________

3. ______________________________

4. ______________________________

5. ______________________________

6. ______________________________

7. ______________________________

8. ______________________________

9. ______________________________

10. ______________________________

Module 1 Activity 2 Handout

Prioritizing

AFTER

1. ______________________________

2. ______________________________

3. ______________________________

4. ______________________________

5. ______________________________

6. ______________________________

7. ______________________________

8. ______________________________

9. ______________________________

10. ______________________________

Module 1 Activity 2 Handout

ACTIVITY 3: MAXIMIZING THE MOMENTS

Activity Purpose:

The purpose of this activity is to demonstrate how valuable our time is, and how if we aren't careful our time can get away from us without us even realizing that it is gone. Additionally, this activity is designed to help girls assess how they are currently spending their time; if they are productively using time to their advantage or wastefully marking time?

Directions:

Each girl is given two handouts: One is titled **A Busy Life for Kids** and the other is titled **Time Tells All**. Using these two handouts, participants will examine how they currently spend their time as well as determine if they are spending their time wisely.

Instructional Procedures:

1. Open with reciting the Five Star Girl Pledge.
2. Begin with a discussion about time and how valuable our time is. Create a dialogue that deals with whether being too busy is a good thing or a bad thing.
3. Introduce the activity.
4. Pass out the **Busy Life for Kids** and the **Time Tells All** handouts.
5. Discuss the "A Busy Life for Kids" findings by Associated Press, and have the girls compare their busyness to the statistical findings.
6. Be prepared to answer questions about how to fill out the chart on the **Time Tells All** handout.
7. Have a discussion with those who would like to share their discoveries of how they spend their time.
8. Always end the activity with the Five Star Girl Pledge.

Materials Needed:

1. **A Busy Life for Kids** handout
2. **Time Tells All** handout
3. Pens or pencils

Time Tells All

Everyday we engage in a multitude of tasks/activities that claim our attention and monopolize our time. Some of these tasks are necessary, i.e. waking up, brushing our teeth, bathing. Some of these tasks are what we deem as important, i.e. going to school, working, hanging out with our friends. And other tasks are things we do, but they have no real importance at all, i.e. watching music videos, painting our nails, gossiping on the telephone. For the purpose of this activity you are to document how you spend your time during the course of any given day.

HOUR	ACTIVITY	(RATE ACTIVITY) Necessary (N) Important (I) Not Important (NI)
6:00 a.m.		
7:00 a.m.		
8:00 a.m.		
9:00 a.m.		
10:00 a.m.		
11:00 a.m.		
12:00 p.m.		
1:00 p.m.		
2:00 p.m.		
3:00 p.m.		
4:00 p.m.		
5:00 p.m.		
6:00 p.m.		
7:00 p.m.		
8:00 p.m.		
9:00 p.m.		
10:00 p.m.		
11:00 p.m.		
12:00 a.m.		

Module 1 Activity 3 Handout

A Busy Life for Kids

About 80 percent of middle and high school students participate in organized activities after school and on weekends, and most have something scheduled nearly every day.

Middle and high school student participation in organized activities outside school hours:

Frequency

Everyday or almost ever day
57%

A couple days a week
37%

School days and weekends
79%

Types of Activities

Sports
66%

School clubs or activities
62%

Volunteer work
60%

Religious institution/church group
54%

Lessons (incl. music, dance, art)
52%

After-school program
52%

Part-time job
37%

Tutoring/academic/test preparation
30%

Organization (e.g. Scouts)
19%

Parents' best reason for child to be involved in organized activities outside school hours:

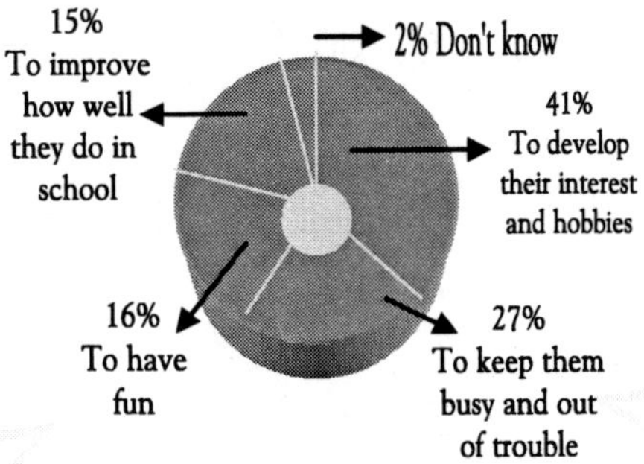

Module 1 Activity 3 Handout

Module Two: Values & Virtue

Five Star Girl Quote:
"Deal with yourself as an individual worthy of respect and make everyone else deal with you the same way."
Nikki Giovanni

Module Goals:

1. To define genuine value.
2. To build self worth by way of establishing standards and boundaries.
3. To demonstrate how value over time becomes virtue.

Module Overview:

Living in a society filled with contradictions, and living amidst so many individuals who ascribe to rather than retreat from these contradictions can make the most astute among us wonder. We think we know better, yet we still find ourselves wondering if the shift in our society's thinking is right and we're wrong. We hear that women who wear too many clothes are too conservative, while women who wear not enough clothes are too provocative. We hear that smoking can cause cancer, yet we see advertisements of women in seductive attire inviting us to participate in the destruction of our own health. For ages girls who date more than one guy are looked down upon and called scandalous, while guys who date more than one girl are applauded and called "the man".

While the contradictions are seemingly, endless that which combats the weightiness of such contradictions is an understanding of our worth and value as well as an establishment of clear cut standards and boundaries that we will live by regardless of what society says or does. Although it does happen more often than not, other peoples' confusion does not have to become our confusion. Even at an early age, girls can develop and adhere to a moral code that insulates them from destructive vices like premature or unsafe sex, experimenting with drugs/alcohol, hooking school, and/or participating in criminal activity. In fact, the earlier such a standard is set the more secure one becomes in their sense of self worth and less likely will be the chances of anything or anyone penetrating through.

Module Activities:

1. Building a Secure Me
2. Throne Life
3. Final Hour
4. This I Know . . .

Fact Finding:

- **Because girls are nurtured more in the process of their development, their value systems tend to be more defined than that of their male counterparts. (Farrell 1993)**

Activity 1: Building a Secure Me

Activity Purpose:

The purpose of this activity is to build upon the foundation setting process by erecting a value structure that will serve as a model of how the girls will conduct their lives.

Directions:

Each girl will be given a pile of popsicle sticks, some craft glue, and a black permanent marker. The craft glue and markers can be shared amongst the girls. The girls are then instructed via a visual demonstration how to begin to build upon their perspective foundations using the popsicle sticks and the craft glue. They can make as many floors as necessary, and upon the development of the various floors they must label them.

Instructional Procedures:

1. Open with reciting the Five Star Girl Pledge.
2. Begin with a brief reiteration of the solid foundation discussion.
3. Go on to discuss the building process and how having a strong foundation is one thing, but in order for the structure to be fully secure and stable one must be just as mindful about what is placed upon the foundation.
4. Introduce activity and give step by step directions.
5. Have each girl talk about what their structure is made of and how they hope to stay guided by their stated values.
6. Always end the activity with the Five Star Girl Pledge.

Materials Needed:

1. Popsicle sticks
2. Craft glue
3. Permanent markers (black)

ACTIVITY 2: THRONE LIFE

Activity Purpose:

The purpose of this activity is to acquaint the girls with queens who reigned with power and authority. Additionally, this activity will engage participants around the attributes needed to be a young lady of queenly standing.

Directions:

Each girl will be given the **Throne Life** handout and asked to complete it to the best of their ability. The facilitator is responsible for having done some preliminary research and reading about the Great African Queens being presented so that he/she can knowledgeably lead a discussion about power, respect, truth, gracefulness, courage, authority, and wisdom.

Instructional Procedures:

1. Open with reciting the Five Star Girl Pledge.
2. Begin with a discussion about queens from all around the world. Talk about how a woman became a queen years ago, what it was like to reign as a queen, etc.
3. Ask the participants what they know about queens, whether from school work or from reading they perhaps did on their own.
4. Introduce the activity and give step by step directions.
5. Distribute the **Throne Life** handout.
6. Go over the girls' answers and their knowledge of the Great African Queens.
7. Always end the activity with the Five Star Girl Pledge.

Materials Needed:

1. **Throne Life** handout
2. Pen or pencil

Throne Life

Queens exists all over the world. The introduction of the Dare to Be Queen Curriculum opens with a brief overview of some prominent queens. As participants of the Dare to Be Queen model you are aspiring to acquire queenly attributes that will make you Five Star Girls—girls who are at the top of their game and at the head of their class; girls who believe in themselves and want only the best for themselves. Below are seven Great African Queens, see if you can match their name with their reign and history.

Cleopatra VII - Queen of Egypt (69-30 B.C.) The most famous of seven matriachs to bear this name, Cleopatra rose to the throne at seventeen. The young queen is often erroneously portrayed as Caucasian, however, she was of both Greek and African descent. ______

1

Nefertari - Nubian Queen of Egypt (1292-1225 B.C.) One of the many great Nubian queens, Nefertari is heralded as the queen who wed for peace. Her marriage to King Rameses II of Egypt, one of the last great Egyptian Pharaohs, began strictly as a political move, a sharing of power between two leaders. ______

2

Nandi - Queen of Zululand (1778-1826) The story of Nandi is a story of courage and steadfast devotion. To this day, the zulu people use her name, "Nandi," to refer to a woman of high esteem. ______

3

Nzingha - Amazon Queen of Matamba, West Africa (1582-1663) Many women ranked among the great rulers of Africa including this Angolan queen who was an astute diplomat and excelled as a military leader. ______

4

Makeda- Queen of Sheba (960 B.C.) "She gave the king 120 talents of gold, and of spices very great store and precious stones; there came no more abundance of spices as these which the Queen of Sheba gave to King Solomon." (Kings, 10:10). The Biblical passage refers to the gifts Makeda presented King Solomon of Israel on her famed journey to visit the Judean monarc. But Makeda's gifts to Solomon extended beyond material objects; she also gave him a son, Menelek. ______

5

Queen Amina of Zaria (1588-1589) The elder daughter of Bakwa Turunku, who founded the Zazzau Kingdom in 1536, queen Amina came to power between 1588 and 1589 A.D. Unlike her younger sister, Zariya (from whom the city of Zaria drives its name), Amina is generally rembered for her fierce military exploits. ______

6

Yaa Asantewa - Queen of Ghana (1863-1923) Queen mother Yaa Asantewa led her nation in the last Ashanti war against the British when her country was called "The Gold Coast". Yaa Asantewa's name and bravery will always be remembered, because of her agitation the return of Prempeh was coverted into stirring demands for independence. ______

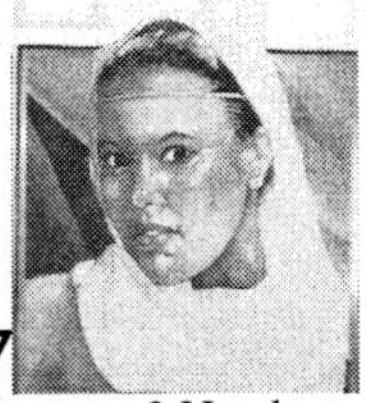
7

Activity 3: Final Hour

Activity Purpose:

The purpose of this activity is to engage girls' thinking around the message of Lauryn Hill's *Final Hour* song and what the song's message is to us.

Directions:

The facilitator will play Lauryn Hill's *Final Hour* song from The Miseducation of Lauryn Hill CD and create a discussion around the questions on the **A Look Into the Final Hour** handout.

Instructional Procedures:

1. Open with reciting the Five Star Girl Pledge.
2. Begin by letting the participants know that you are getting ready to listen to Lauryn Hill's *Final Hour* song.
3. Ask the participants if they've heard the song before.
4. Play the song *Final Hour.* (Play time 4:45)
5. Engage the girls with the questions made available on the **A Look Into the Final Hour** handout.
6. Always end the activity with the Five Star Girl Pledge.

Materials Needed:

1. CD Player
2. The Miseducation of Lauryn Hill CD
3. **A Look Into the Final Hour** handout

A Look Into the Final Hour

As the girls listen to Lauryn Hill's Final Hour, write the following questions on a blackboard or on a flip chart. After the song finishes playing indulge the girls with the questions.

1. What is the final hour?

2. What does Lauryn Hill mean by *"you can get the money, you can get the power, keep your eyes on the final hour"*?

3. What does the statement *"it ain't about what you cop, its about what you keep"* mean?

4. Was there anything else that stuck out for you in this song?

5. How does the *Final Hour* and **values** go together?

ACTIVITY 4: WHAT I KNOW FOR SURE

Activity Purpose:

The purpose of this activity is to have the girls look introspectively at those things that they know for certain; those things that keep them connected to their values and will essentially help them to cultivate their virtue.

Directions:

The facilitator will lead a discussion about life; and the need to be anchored and grounded in a belief that can withstand tough, trying times. After which, participants will assess their anchors as they complete the **Things I Know for Sure** handout.

Instructional Procedures:

1. Open with reciting the Five Star Girl Pledge.
2. Begin with a dialogue about life, and how life has the capacity to knock us around, send us some disappointments, or surprise us with unexpected blessings.
3. Share with the girls that those of us who are able to make progress, stay encouraged, and maintain our strength, due so by way of some things…some truths that we have stored in the confines of our hearts and minds. Tell them that these things represent the things we "know for sure."
4. Introduce and distribute the **Things I Know for Sure** handout.
5. Give the girls 15 minutes to do the handout, and then allow those girls who would like to an opportunity to share.
6. Always end the activity with the Five Star Girl Pledge.

Materials Needed:

1. **Things I Know for Sure** handout
2. Pens or pencils

Things I Know For Sure

As we go through life, the bumps, the obstacles, the difficulties and even the tragedies we will encounter are destined to shake our foundations and in doing so will attempt to challenge who we say we are. If we are to withstand the bumps, overcome the obstacles, and deal with the difficulties there are some things we must know for sure. These things will help us to hang in there when we don't feel like it; they will give us strength when we are weak; they will ward off doubt, but ultimately these things that "we know for sure" will cause us to triumph—time and time again. For the purpose of this activity, you will finish the existing statement with what you know for sure.

1. I know that I can do anything because . . .

2. I refuse to allow anyone to make me think less of myself because . . .

3. When I am down I know that I can count on ____________________ to pick me up because . . .

4. I am most proud of the fact that I . . .

5. My greatest weapon when doing warfare with my mind is . . .

6. That one thing that has more power over me than it should is . . .

Module 2 Activity 4 Handout

Module Three: My Body . . . My Business

Five Star Girl Quote:
"Examine the label you apply to yourself. Every label is a boundary or limit you will not let yourself cross." Dwayne Dyer

Module Goals:

1. To teach the importance of girls tending to their physical health.
2. To introduce healthy and practical ways to nourish and preserve the body.

Module Overview:

Youthfulness does not always have a regard for fruitfulness. There is an overwhelming perception among young people, erroneous though it may be, that they can and will outlive time. There is this belief that time and years will somehow not catch up to them. Indeed this thinking has everything to do with an ignorance and an innocence that is common to being young and unable to see beyond one's youthfulness. This explanation alone, however, does not and cannot negate the need for young people to take their physical health more seriously.

While this ignorance exists among young people, to some degree, across the board, the ignorance that rests upon girls is even more alarming because it is intertwined with and exacerbated by false and flawed images of womanhood, beauty, and what boys want their girlfriends to look like. We have girls on one end of the spectrum who want so badly to fit society's image of beauty that they will eat little to nothing, starve themselves, exercise until they pass out and end up underweight; while girls on the other end of the spectrum have simply given up on the notion that they will ever meet society's criteria of beauty and as a result over indulge in food, consume unhealthy amounts of fattening snacks, never exercise, and end up overweight. It is important, therefore, that girls have a realistic understanding of what constitutes healthy for their individual bodies. It is equally important that girls are adequately educated about the long-term ramifications of altering, enhancing, decorating or neglecting their bodies; ramifications that can quite possibly follow them into their adult years.

Module Activities:

1. Campaign for the Cause
2. You Are What You Eat
3. Real Women Have Curves

Fact Finding:

- **Girls' weight and dieting concerns are linked more strongly to social and psychological issues than to physical health matters. Cross-sectional studies have shown weight and eating concerns to correlate with decreased self-esteem and increased depression. Participants in qualitative studies thought that looking good, which means having an appropriate body size, is important to attracting boyfriends. In another study, where teenage girls were asked to give one or more reasons for dieting, 95% listed cosmetic reasons while only 25% gave health-related reasons.**

__Gwen Chapman__, Ph.D., School of Family and Nutritional Sciences, University of British Columbia.

ACTIVITY 1: CAMPAIGN FOR THE CAUSE

Activity Purpose:

The purpose of this activity is to have girls take a responsible stand about four major issues affecting their physical and nutritional health by having them develop creative marketing campaigns. Additionally, this activity will allow girls to develop their comfort level with working in groups.

Directions:

Divide girls into groups of four. Each group will be given the task of developing a marketing campaign around one of four topics dealing with physical or nutritional health.

Instructional Procedures:

1. Open with reciting the Five Star Girl Pledge.
2. Begin by dividing the girls into groups of four.
3. Assign each group a topic from which they will develop their campaign around.
4. The topics are: Obesity, Anorexia, Physical Fitness and Eating Right.
5. Distribute the **Campaign for the Cause** handout which lists all of the rules for the group, a piece of flip chart size paper, a marker and possibly some tape.
6. The groups have 30 minutes to develop their campaign in preparation for presenting it to the masses.
7. While the groups are working, walk around the room to see how things are progressing. See if anyone needs clarification about what they have to do.
8. Always end the activity with the Five Star Girl Pledge.

Materials Needed:

1. Flip chart size paper
2. Markers
3. Tape
4. **Campaign for the Cause** handout

Campaign for the Cause

Every *good* idea becomes a *great* idea because it is marketed to a population of people who buy into the idea. Thousands of people are helped every year because one person or one group of persons came up with something other people could benefit from. For the purpose of this activity your group is to develop a very creative marketing campaign to address the topic your group was assigned. Remember to be unique and different. Think outside the box, yet not so far out the box that others cannot appreciate where you are coming from.

____

Your Group's Topic

Rules for developing your campaign:

1. Your campaign must be creative and innovative.
2. You must select a group captain.
3. You must develop a slogan.
4. You must have a targeted audience.
5. You must have a clear mission. (What you want this campaign to accomplish.)
6. You must have clear goals. (How you will accomplish what you say you will.)
7. You must indicate what your marketing/promotional materials will be.
8. You must be prepared to give a 5 minute presentation of your marketing campaign.

Module 3 Activity 1 Handout

ACTIVITY 2: YOU ARE WHAT YOU EAT

Activity Purpose:

The purpose of this activity is to introduce girls to the major food groups, test their knowledge about these groups, and encourage them to incorporate healthy food intake into their eating routines.

Directions:

Each girl will receive an empty Food Guide Pyramid handout along with the pieces that fit into each group. The girls will then be asked to see how many they can appropriately place in the correct position.

Instructional Procedures:

1. Open with reciting the Five Star Girl Pledge.
2. Begin by discussing nutrition and how important it is for all of us to eat healthy. Make certain that you include in the discussion how what we eat really becomes a core part of who we are—from a physical perspective.
3. Again, the facilitator would need to have done some preliminary studying in preparation for this activity.
4. Distribute the blank **Food Guide Pyramid** handout along with the food group categories.
5. Instruct the girls to see how many they can place appropriately on the Food Guide Pyramid.
6. Allow approximately 20 minutes for them to do this on their own, then show them your large Food Guide Pyramid with the categories filled in.
7. Before ending the activity distribute to each girl a copy of the completed **Food Guide Pyramid** handout and encourage them to talk with their parents about learning to eat nutritionally healthy so that they can ultimately be physically healthy.
8. Always end the activity with the Five Star Girl Pledge.

Materials Needed:

1. Blank **Food Guide Pyramid** handout
2. Food group categories
3. Completed **Food Guide Pyramid** handout
4. Pen or pencil

The Food Guide Pyramid

The Pyramid is an outline of what to eat each day. It's not a rigid prescription, but a general guide that lets you choose a healthful diet that's right for you.

The Pyramid calls for eating a variety of foods to get the nutrients you need and at the same time the right amount of calories to maintain or improve your weight.

The Pyramid also focuses on fat because most Americans' diets are too high in fat, especially saturated fat.

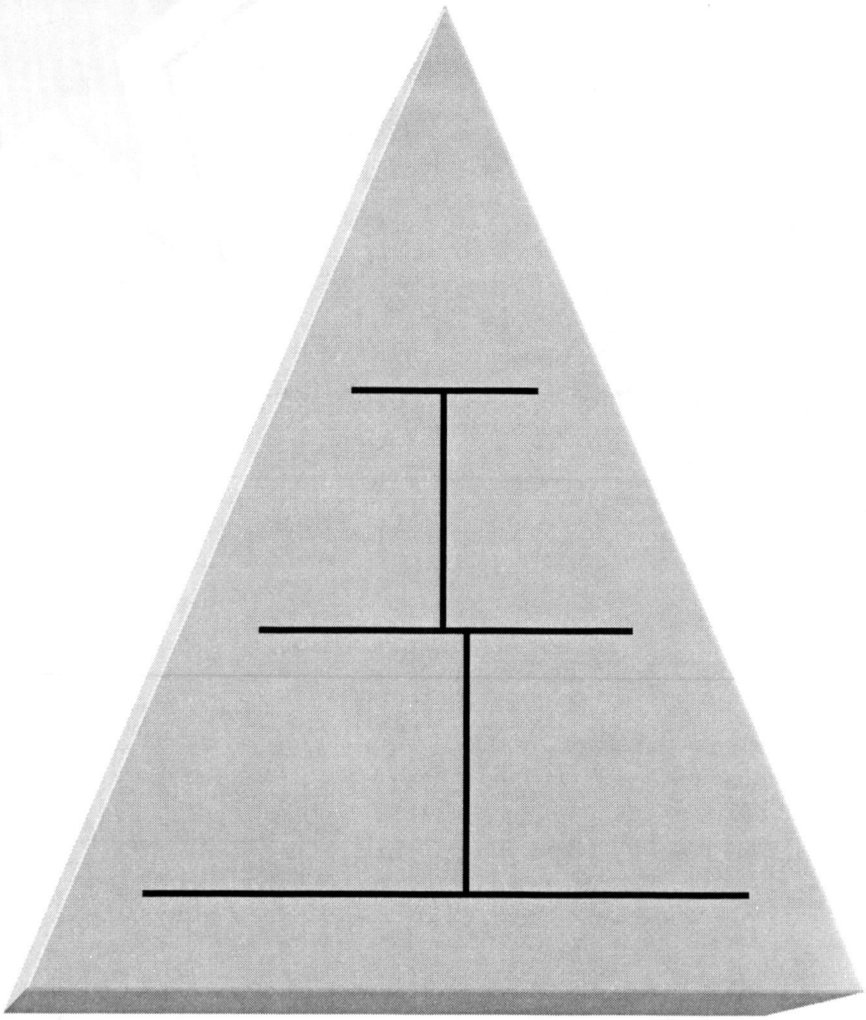

Module 3 Activity 2 Handout

Food Categories

Fats, Oils & Sweets
USE SPARINGLY

Milk, Yogurt,
& Cheese Group
2-3 SERVINGS

Meat, Poultry, Fish,
Dry Beans, Eggs
& Nuts Group
2 -3 SERVINGS

Fruit
Group
2-4 SERVINGS

Bread, Cereal,
Rice & Pasta
Group
6-11 SERVINGS

Module 3 Activity 2 Handout

What's the Best Nutrition Advice?

The best nutrition advice is following the Dietary Guidelines for Americans. There are seven guidelines for a healthful diet—advice for healthy Americans 2 years of age or more. By following the Dietary Guidelines, you can enjoy better healthy and reduce your chances of getting certain diseases. These Guidelines, developed jointly by USDA and HHS, are the best, most up-to-date advice from nutrition scientists and are the basis of Federal nutrition policy.

Module 3 Activity 2 Handout

Activity 3: Real Women Have Curves

Activity Purpose:

The purpose of this activity is to allow girls to view a movie about a young Latino girl who was able to maintain a level of pride about her body despite the fact that she was somewhat overweight. Additionally, it is hoped that the message of the movie will inspire and encourage participants to recognize their own beauty even when others don't.

Directions:

View and discuss the movie **Real Women Have Curves.** Have the girls answer the questions on the **Real Women Have Curves** handout after the movie has been viewed. Finally, discuss the answers from the handout as well as entertain any other helpful exchange the girls might need to have. (The viewing of this movie may have to be done in two different meetings because of the running time.)

Instructional Procedures:

1. Open with reciting the Five Star Girl Pledge.
2. Begin by letting the girls know that you all are about to watch a movie about a Latino young lady who faces constant criticism about her weight, but handles it like a champ.
3. Distribute the **Real Women Have Curves** handout and ask the girls to see how many answers in Part I they can fill in. Direct them not to do Part II of the handout until after the movie.
4. View **Real Women Have Curves.** (Running time: 88 minutes)
5. After the movie ends have the girls take 10 minutes to answer the questions in Part II of the handout.
6. Once the 10 minutes are up have those girls who would like to share discuss their answers with the group.
7. Always end the activity with the Five Star Girl Pledge.

Materials Needed:

1. Television
2. DVD Player
3. The movie ***Real Women Have Curves***
4. **Real Women Have Curves** handout
5. Pens or pencils

Real Women Have Curves

As you review the movie, *Real Women Have Curves*, indicate who said the following statements to whom.

Part I.

1. "She hates me. She thinks I'm ugly and fat."

_____________________ said this to ____________________

2. "Pretty dresses aren't just for skinny girls."

_____________________ said this to ____________________

3. "I already found it. You are my gold."

_____________________ said this to ____________________

4. "Turn the lights on. I want you to see me. This is what I look like."

_____________________ said this to ____________________

5. "You're not bad looking, you're just overweight."

_____________________ said this to ____________________

6. "Look at you – you look awful."

_____________________ said this to ____________________

7. Don't even think about it. You'll never fit into that."

_____________________ said this to ____________________

8. "Come on out and give me your blessing."

_____________________ said this to ____________________

Module 3 Activity 3 Handout

Real Women Have Curves

Now that you have viewed the movie, *Real Women Have Curves*, answer the following questions.

Part II.

1. Why did Ana initially shy aware from the idea of college?

2. What upset Ana about them making the dresses for $18.00 and the store selling the dresses for $600.00?

3. Why do you think Ana's mother insisted on saying negative, hurtful things to Ana about her appearance and her weight?

4. Would you say Ana had low self esteem, high self esteem, or average self esteem?

5. Who was Mr. Guzman, and how did he make a difference in Ana's life?

6. What was the message Ana conveyed to the other women at her job when she convinced them to take their clothes off?

7. In your opinion, why was Ana so proud of her body?

8. How, if at all, did the movie inspire you?

Module 3 Activity 3 Handout

MODULE FOUR: SEALING THE SACRED

Five Star Girl Quote:
My body is a precious temple. Therefore, I will cherish and respect it as such."
Mischa Green

MODULE GOALS:

1. To discuss the physical developmental process and how it impacts a girl's desire for sex.
2. To teach girls how to protect their minds and their bodies around the matter of sex.
3. To introduce realistic strategies for warding off the temptation to engage in premature sexual activity.

MODULE OVERVIEW:

One of the most trying aspects of early puberty--trying for both parent and child is the gap between a girl's physical development and her psychological development. For a young girl, having a well-developed body can raise the stakes at a time when rebellion is becoming the norm. A teenage girl, who has the physical equipment but not the emotional maturity, can turn to sex to prove her independence, often with disastrous results, says Andrew Goldstein, an obstetrician-gynecologist who teaches at Johns Hopkins University in Baltimore. The pull and the press to engage in premature sexual activity is therefore very real for many girls, and must be addressed in a very real way.

We must begin addressing this delicate issue by engaging girls in a realistic dialogue that both validates their physical desires and at the same time introduces them to the psychological impact often associated with allowing their body to take them places their mind isn't quite prepared to go. Adult women must make themselves and their stories more available to girls. As a society, we must be more responsible and accountable for the inappropriate and seductive messages we sent to girls—daily. As parents, we must be better prepared to listen, hear, understand and redirect our girls around the issue of sex. Ultimately, girls must be exceptional stewards of their bodies and of their minds. They must make safe, educated, quality decisions that are reflective of the promising future they desire to have.

MODULE ACTIVITIES:

1. Role Play: You Should Have Known Better
2. Stairway to Love & Respect – Without Sex
3. Straight Talkin' Roundtable

FACT FINDING:

- According to a 1999 report by Kaiser Family Foundation, two thirds of primetime television programs feature sexual content, and an average of five scenes per hour depict sexual talk or behavior.
- A National Campaign to Prevent Teen Pregnancy report notes that music videos objectify women--no surprise there--with 57 percent of women appearing partially clothed compared with 28 percent of the men.

ACTIVITY 1: YOU SHOULD HAVE KNOWN BETTER

Activity Purpose:

The purpose of this to have girls actually act out a role play scenario that can and does happen in high schools cross this country everyday so as engage girls around appropriate sex related decision making skills.

Directions:

Enter into a discussion with the girls about the topic sex. Tell them how important it is—for their own physical and emotional well being—that they have a healthy mindset about the matter of sex. Then let the girls know you all are about to embark upon a role play (explain what a role play is) that involves the tough issue of sex.

Instructional Procedures:

1. Open with reciting the Five Star Girl Pledge.
2. Begin by entering into a discussion with the girls about sex. Perhaps ask how many of them are still virgins? Ask if they have a responsible adult in their lives that they can talk about sex with? Get a sense of their level of comfort or discomfort.
3. Assure them that although sex is a difficult topic, its one that must be talked about if girls are going to make responsible decisions about who they share their bodies with.
4. Introduce the **Role Play: You Should Have Known Better** activity by telling the girls what a role play is.
5. Give the girls the handout, allow them 15 minutes to put the role play together and 10 minutes to act it out.
6. After the role play, engage the girls about the approach they took and the way they handled the tasks of the role play.
7. Always end the activity with the "Five Star Girl Pledge".

Materials Needed:

1. **Role Play: You Should Have Known Better** handout

You Should Have Known Better

Tia and Maria are 11th grade best friends. They've been best friends since 3rd grade. Maria knows like the rest of the school that there is a guy on the basketball team named Todd who has the hots for her best friend Tia. For months Maria has been warning Tia to stay away from the Todd because Maria thinks he's no good for Tia. Tia also thinks that this guy could be bad news because she's seen him with a lot of different girls during the course of the school year and the school year is only mid way through.

At lunch Tia and Maria have a conversation about Todd because Maria overheard Todd telling one of his team mates that he was going to get Tia. Initially Tia was listening to Maria and feeling her concern—after all they've been best friends for over 8 years and Maria has never told her anything wrong. But, out of nowhere Tia decides that she no longer wants to hear what Maria has to say. As Maria was talking, Tia interrupted her and told her to shut up and mind her business. Tia went on to tell Maria that she likes Todd and he is not the dog everybody is making him out to be. Tia also told Maria that she is not a little girl and she can handle herself on her own. Shortly after saying what she had to say, Tia got up from the table and walked away from Maria. Although Maria was hurt and disappointed, she just let Tia go.

Not one week after their falling out in the cafeteria, a rumor begins to spread around the school that Tia had sex with Todd in the boys' locker room. Everywhere Tia walks someone is snickering and talking about her. With no place else to turn, and feeling quite embarrassed to find out that Todd actually is the dog everybody said he was, Tia turns to Maria for comfort. Tia feels low and violated because she made Todd promise that he wouldn't tell anybody before they had sex and he said that he wouldn't.

You are Maria, Tia's best friend, do you forget about the cafeteria scene and give Tia the comfort she needs, fuss her out, turn your back on her, or do you find Todd and tell him how disgusting he is for being so immature?

Module 4 Activity 1 Handout

ACTIVITY 2: STAIRWAY TO LOVE & RESPECT – WITHOUT SEX

Activity Purpose:

The purpose of this activity is to teach girls that love and respect is more important than sex, and how if your mate loves and respects you he will be less likely to pressure you for sex.

Directions:

Enter into a discussion with the girls about love and respect, and how every relationship has to have these two components as its foundation. Introduce the girls to the **Stairway to Love & Respect – Without Sex** handout, and have each girl discuss where her current relationship is on the stairway.

Instructional Procedures:

1. Open with reciting the Five Star Girl Pledge.
2. Begin by entering into a discussion with the girls about love and respect. Share with the girls that love and respect cannot be optional; and that in fact they are actually mandatory when we talk about having solid, trusting relationships.
3. Poll the girls to see who among them feels like they are in a loving, respectful relationship. Ask them how do they know?
4. Distribute the **Stairway to Love & Respect – Without Sex** handout.
5. Give the girls about 5 minutes to read over the handout.
6. Select five different girls to read each step and then thoroughly discuss them.
7. Ask the girls to define love and define respect in their terms. Talk about love and respect's relevance to preserving one's body.
8. Always end the activity with the Five Star Girl Pledge.

Materials Needed:

1. **Stairway to Love & Respect – Without Sex** handout

Stairway to Love & Respect – Without Sex

Love and respect are essential components of a relationship. These components are that which serve as the foundation of a relationship. This activity demonstrates the Five Steps to Love & Respect – separate and a part from sex. As you read through the steps, ask yourself where your relationship stands. If by chance you do not fall anywhere on this staircase, you must really examine the safety or the authenticity of the relationship you are currently in.

Fifth Step:
Your trust begins to turn into something more. You really, really, really like him. And he really, really, really likes you. The big "L" word has even been floating around throughout some conversations, yet you both have made a commitment to explore *all* of the other ways you can get to know each other *without* having sex.

Fourth Step:
Your parents are accepting of the idea of your boyfriend coming over to visit as long as they are home and his parents feel the same. He respects the boundaries you've expressed about touching, and you feel you can trust him. He adds no pressure. He simply does whatever he can to make you comfortable.

Third Step:
You've consented to the idea of a boyfriend-girlfriend relationship. You feel pretty comfortable with him. You enjoy talking to him. He treats you respectfully. You have a good time together. The dates are more frequent. There is a peck or kiss here and there. You are convinced he's a good guy.

Second Step:
You and the young man have developed a regular routine of talking on the phone. You send endearing and/or silly text messages and e-mails during the course of the day. You may have even gone to see a movie or two—without any kissing. There is some buzz about a boyfriend-girlfriend relationship.

First Step:
You have met a young man. He appears to be pretty cool. There is the possibility of interest on both of your parts. You exchange smiles, some personal information i.e. name age, grade, school, as well as phone numbers. You ask around, he has a clean reputation and appears to be well liked.

Module 4 Activity 2 Handout

ACTIVITY 3: STRAIGHT TALKIN'

Activity Purpose:

The purpose of this activity is to have an open, honest roundtable discussion about abstinence and how girls can successfully maintain a dignified, graceful life of celibacy while living in a sexually provocative, womanizing society.

Directions:

Invite 3 – 4 women from the community i.e. a school teacher, a professor of psychology, social work or public health, a woman minister, an affluent "grounded" business woman, or a pediatrician to join you, the facilitator, at the table with your group of girls. Share with the invited guests that you are inviting them to a roundtable with middle and/or high school age girls to talk about abstinence as well as the physical, emotional and psychological ramifications of premature sex. Make certain that the women are open-minded, compassionate, non-judgmental, and understand the significance of making an investment in young girls.

Instructional Procedures:

1. Open with reciting the Five Star Girl Pledge.
2. The preliminary work of preparing for this activity should actually happen 3-4 weeks in advance.
3. The facilitator is responsible for gathering together 3 - 4 knowledgeable and concerned women to join him/her at the table for a roundtable discussion with the girls.
4. Calls need to be made to potential invited guests to learn of their interest and availability. Once the invitation has been accepted, follow-up letters of confirmation should be mailed. And reminder calls should be made the day before.
5. Do your best to get the girls excited about the roundtable. Tell them that it will be fun. Let them know that this is for them; this is their opportunity to speak their mind as well as get some answers.
6. Be mindful to send thank you notes or letters to invited guests.
7. Always end the activity with the Five Star Girl Pledge.

Materials Needed:

1. Invited Roundtable Guests
2. A nice size room with a table and comfortable chairs
3. Water, juice, cookies or chips

Straight Talkin' Roundtable Facilitator's Guide

Purpose: To have an open, honest roundtable discussion about abstinence and how girls can successfully maintain a dignified, graceful life of celibacy while living in a sexually provocative, womanizing society.

Objective:
1. To provide a healthy forum for girls to ask important questions, get real answers and feel a sense of safety while doing it.
2. To place role models in the form of positive, successful women within arms reach of girls who otherwise may not have any.
3. To replace girls' preoccupation for premature sex with more productive alternatives.

Roundtable Rules: (These rules apply to everyone coming to the table. Anyone who feels that they cannot adhere to these rules can be allowed to excuse herself immediately.)

1. Give a formal welcome to thank everyone for coming.
2. After the welcome, but before reiterating the purpose of the Straight Talkin' Roundtable, have everyone introduce herself. It may also be advantageous to have participants wear stick-on name badges.
3. Reiterate the purpose of the Straight Talkin' Roundtable.
4. Ask participants to honor confidentiality—meaning everything that's said at the table stays at the table.
5. Remind participants to show respect by not talking when someone else is talking.
6. Inform the girls, if it is the case, that there are persons who serve in the capacity of "mandatory reporters" at the table, which means if something is shared of an illegal or life-threatening nature appropriate authorities—including parents will have to be notified.

Module 4 Activity 2 Handout

MODULE FIVE: A SCHOLAR I AM

Five Star Girl Quote:
"Education is your passport to the future, for tomorrow belongs to the people who prepare for it today."
Malcolm X

MODULE GOALS:

1. To teach girls the value of having a solid education.
2. To have girls look at the educational process as one that extends beyond the school setting.
3. To introduce unconventional ways in which education is acquired.

MODULE OVERVIEW:

Smart is relative. Everyone has some degree of intellect and/or academic ability. Going to school everyday, completing class assignments, doing homework, and scoring high on standardized test is not all there is to the educational process. Education comes in a variety of forms. Book knowledge is a form of being educated. Street smarts is a form of being educated. Personal experience is yet another form of acquiring education. While is it mandatory that our girls get all they can from the classroom experience. While we want our girls to pursue the highest level of academia their hearts desire. While we encourage having great study habits; we equally encourage a well balanced educational experience that is as wholesome as it is rewarding.

When introducing the idea of an education to girls we must therefore begin with the big picture (life) as opposed to the small picture (school). We must instill in our girls a desire to reach a level of success that is not continuously confined to a classroom. By introducing a broader meaning of education to girls, we advertently teach them how to acquire, master and use intelligence on a more exhaustive level; a level that serves to benefit them in particular and humanity in general—for this is what a true scholar is.

It is believed that once girls understand, from the very beginning, the utilitarian aspect of an education across the continuum of life, they will have more of an appreciation for and a commitment to the educational process.

MODULE ACTIVITIES:

1. Lobbying to Learn . . . Learning to Lobby
2. Urban Leadership Excursion
3. Criss Cross Word Toss

FACT FINDING:

- **Because teachers assume girls will be conscientious students, they tend to encourage boys more often by commenting on their work, offering suggestions, and giving praise (Elium & Elium, 1994 p. 73).**
- **Cognitive development affects how children perceive and interpret the information they are presented, thus making it difficult for them to excel if cognitive development is impeded (Grimm-Wasil, 1994)**

ACTIVITY 1: LOBBYING TO LEARN . . . LEARNING TO LOBBY

Activity Purpose:

The purpose of this activity is to teach girls how to lobby on behalf of their education process.

Directions:

By way of writing letters and creating protest signs, girls will learn the importance of letting their voices be heard about issues affecting their present as well as their future.

Instructional Procedures:

1. Open with reciting the Five Star Girl Pledge.
2. The facilitator will open with a dialogue about how important it is for people to know how to speak up for themselves. You will also talk about the power of the group, and how many collective voices saying the same thing can bring about powerful change.
3. The girls will then be given the scenario that the mayor is putting on a Town Hall Meeting about Education in three weeks, and in preparation for the town hall meeting you want them to address letters to the mayor stating their dissatisfaction with their educational process and/or setting i.e. unclean schools, dull lights, outdated textbooks, impatient teachers, over-capacity classrooms, etc.
4. The girls will also be instructed that in addition to writing letters, they will be creating protest signs to carry in front of City Hall on the day of the Town Hall Meeting.

5. Distribute the **Sample Lobby Letter** handout along with paper for the girls to write their letters on.
6. Once the girls have completed writing their letters, distribute the **Sample Lobby Sign** handout along with poster board for the girls to design or craft their lobby signs.
7. Always end the activity with the Five Star Girl Pledge.

Materials Needed:

1. Paper
2. Pens or pencils
3. Poster board
4. Markers

SAMPLE LOBBY LETTER

January 1, 2005

The Honorable Mayor Joe Doe
City Hall
500 City Street
Mayortown, MD 21201

Dear Mayor Doe:

1st Paragraph – Introduce yourself…tell your name, your age, what part of town you live in and where you go to school.

2nd Paragraph – State your concern about the educational system in general and/or your concern about the educational environment at your school in particular. Also explain, from your perspective, how your ability to learn is impacted by the fact that certain things are not in place as they ought to be.

3rd Paragraph – Suggest some changes that you would like to see take place to resolve the concerns you voiced in paragraph 2. And thank the mayor in advance for giving his/her attention to your concern.

Sincerely,

Jane Doe
Queens High School, 10th Grader

Module 5 Activity 1 Handout

SAMPLE LOBBY SIGN

Using the poster board and markers provided, draw or craft your own lobby sign. Remember, this sign represents *your voice* and should uniquely express *your feelings* about *your education.*

Module 5 Activity 1 Handout

Activity 2: Urban Leadership Excursion

Activity Purpose:

The purpose of this activity is to instill in girls a concept of community involvement that will awaken their leadership potential as well as help them understand the value of giving back.

Directions:

Led by the facilitator, girls will embark upon a community involvement endeavor that represents some aspect of giving back or investing in people less fortunate than themselves.

Instructional Procedures:

1. Open with reciting the Five Star Girl Pledge.
2. Begin this activity with a discussion about community involvement and why it is necessary for everybody to give back and make an investment of their time, their talent or their finances into the lives of those who may not be as fortunate as they are.
3. Highlight the fact that all great leaders began by serving. (Be prepared to give some examples.)
4. Share with the girls that you all, as a group, will collectively choose a community program or school to share your time and talents with.
5. Read to the girls the list of places you've looked into and collectively, by a general consensus, decide where you all will go.
6. Following the actual urban leadership excursion, have the girls discuss how, why, and if the experience impacted their lives.
7. Always end the activity with the Five Star Girl Pledge.

Materials Needed:

1. An open mind
2. Compassion
3. A community program or school

Urban Leadership Excursion
Ideas or Suggestions

Below are some ideas or suggestions you may explore for your urban leadership excursion. Please keep in mind that this activity seeks to do the following things: a. develop leaders, b. instill a community involvement interest, and c. expose the girls to the benefits associated with helping, inspiring and encouraging others.

- Visit an elementary school and read to the students.
- Mentor or tutor younger age students
- Visit a shelter and help feed the homeless
- Visit a hospital's children ward or a children's hospital and read to the patients or play games with them
- Visit a senior citizens' center and read to the seniors or play games with them

Module 5 Activity 2 Handout

ACTIVITY 3: CRISS-CROSS WORD TOSS

Activity Purpose:

The purpose of this activity is to have the girls engage in the fun of doing a crossword puzzle while building their vocabulary.

Directions:

Each girl will be given the **Verbal Advantage Crossword Puzzle** handout, and asked to not only find the words but also use the dictionary provided to look up any meanings to words they are not familiar with.

Instructional Procedures:

1. Open with reciting the Five Star Girl Pledge.
2. Let the girls know that this is a vocabulary building activity where they will find the words in the **Verbal Advantage Crossword Puzzle**, and then locate the words they may not be familiar with in a dictionary that will be provided for them.
3. Distribute the **Verbal Advantage Crossword Puzzle** handout.
4. Make certain dictionaries are available and accessible.
5. Always end the activity with the Five Star Girl Pledge.

Materials Needed:

1. **Verbal Advantage Crossword Puzzle** handout
2. Pens or pencils
3. Dictionaries

Verbal Advantage Crossword Puzzle

It's all about expanding and building your vocabulary!

G	J	K	L	D	A	B	S	V	E	T	G	H	R	O	A	S	W
T	E	D	U	C	A	T	I	O	N	A	L	V	S	Q	P	P	T
E	O	E	Q	A	Z	U	W	L	C	I	G	I	V	V	E	M	A
N	W	V	B	H	N	O	E	M	U	D	Y	C	P	T	R	C	N
A	S	T	U	T	E	D	Z	B	M	N	U	I	W	B	F	R	T
C	X	H	O	I	M	V	E	R	B	A	L	S	F	E	U	J	A
I	V	B	E	F	U	D	D	L	E	D	B	S	Y	M	N	R	M
T	W	S	D	O	P	E	U	C	R	O	K	I	V	W	C	U	O
Y	C	C	R	E	D	E	N	C	E	V	G	T	H	W	T	B	U
A	V	E	W	O	N	U	K	K	D	D	P	U	I	O	O	F	N
I	M	P	E	C	C	A	B	L	E	H	G	D	E	D	R	W	T
G	E	S	C	P	Q	U	L	X	C	T	T	E	B	H	Y	O	M
R	V	M	K	E	I	L	H	D	P	R	U	M	I	N	A	T	E
O	Y	S	C	I	R	C	U	M	S	C	R	I	B	E	P	G	K

astute	encumbered	tantamount
befuddled	impeccable	tenacity
credence	perfunctory	verbal
educational	ruminate	vicissitude

Module 5 Activity 3 Handout

Module Six:
Anger Management 101

Five Star Girl Quote:
"As long as you can find someone else to blame for anything you are doing, you cannot be held accountable or responsible for your growth or the lack of it."
Sun Bear

Module Goals:

1. To help girls understand anger.
2. To give girls effective strategies for managing anger.

Module Overview:

Not too many, if any of us will escape life unscathed or unscarred. If we live long enough, we will have the misfortune of someone hurting our feelings, trampling upon our kindness, abusing our trust, and/or taking for granted our value. Regardless of the way in which a violation occur, the disappointment and pain that surfaces as a result of the violation has the capacity to stir up emotions and feelings we sometimes are unable to control or manage. Experiencing different emotions and feelings is healthy; not being able to control or manage what we feel is where the trouble begins. Why? Because when we fail to appropriately deal with our emotions and feelings, our emotions and feelings has a way of dealing with us.

Unfortunately, for many girls this inability to appropriately deal with emotions and feelings tends to have a lot to do with how we are reared as a gender. We are taught to not complain; always think positive; forgive and forget; do not hold grudges; put others feelings before our own. As a result of such a rearing, even when we are mistreated, we still try to hold true to that which we have been told that girls . . . young ladies . . . and women are supposed to do. The truth of the matter is our hurt, disappointment, and distrust does not somehow vanish into thin air because we have ignored it. Rather, it festers and compounds, and over a period of time snowballs into something ugly, something unmanageable, and in some cases, something harmful—either to us or to someone else.

It is, therefore, extremely important that girls are taught how to honestly and realistically validate their feelings with the intent to gain a healthy perspective as well as develop manageable strategies for dealing with uncomfortable and potentially hazardous feelings.

Module Activities:

1. Girlhood
2. Managing Me

Fact Finding:

- **Women who, as girls, never learned to be comfortable with conflict as adults have trouble distinguishing normal, day-to-day disagreements from personal attacks. Gail Evans, Play Like a Man, Win Like a Woman**

ACTIVITY 1: GIRLHOOD

Activity Purpose:

The purpose of this activity is to allow the girls to view the documentary ***Girlhood***, which depicts the lives of two girls who allowed their anger to control their actions.

Directions:

View and discuss the documentary ***Girlhood***. Have the girls answer the questions on the **Girlhood** handout after the documentary has been viewed. Finally, discuss the answers from the handout as well as entertain any other helpful exchange the girls might need to have. (The viewing of this movie may have to be done in two different meetings because of the running time.)

Instructional Procedures:

1. Open with reciting the Five Star Girl Pledge.
2. Begin by letting the girls know that you all are about to watch a documentary about two girls from Baltimore; both of whom allowed their anger to get the best of them, and as a result ended up in Waxter Detention Center, home to Maryland's most violent girl offenders.
3. View ***Girlhood***. (Running time: 82 minutes)
4. After viewing the documentary, have the girls take 10 minutes to answer the questions on the **Girlhood** handout.
5. Once the 10 minutes are up have those girls who would like to share discuss their answers with the group.
6. Always end the activity with the Five Star Girl Pledge.

Materials Needed:

1. Television
2. DVD Player
3. ***Girlhood*** Documentary
4. **Girlhood** handout
5. Pens or pencils

Girlhood

After viewing the documentary ***Girlhood,*** answer the following questions about the two young girls who were featured in the documentary.

SHANAE

1. What caused Shanae to turn to a life of drinking and drugging?
2. What did Shanae do to end up at Waxter Juvenile Facility?
3. In your opinion, did Shanae appear to understand the depth of her violation, or did she take things to lightly?
4. Who helped Shanae the most with getting her life together?
5. What could Shanae have done differently so as not to end up in Waxter Juvenile Facility?
6. How did it make you feel when Shanae's mother died? And do you think you would have handled it as well as Shanae did?

MEGAN

1. What caused Megan to turn to a life of crime and delinquency?
2. What, if anything, were Megan's other options than crime and delinquency?
3. Who would you say Megan was most angry with: her mother, her father, her family or herself? And why?
4. In your opinion, do you think Megan wants to change and be better? Explain your answer?
5. What type of help would you suggest Megan get to deal with her anger?
6. How did you feel about Megan cursing her mother out for the final time? And do you feel that it was justified?

GENERAL QUESTIONS

1. Do you think girls carry anger differently than boys? If so, why?
2. What are some of the ways society perhaps contributes to the anger and delinquency of girls?

Module 6 Activity 1 Handout

ACTIVITY 2: MANAGING ME

Activity Purpose:
The purpose of this activity is to have girls assess their anger triggers and then develop healthy alternatives to deal with these triggers.

Directions:
After a brief discussion about anger and the importance of anger management each girl will be given an **Anger Assessment** handout to honestly evaluate their anger triggers.

Instructional Procedures:
1. Open with reciting the Five Star Girl Pledge.
2. Begin the session with a dialogue about anger—what anger is, why people become angry, and how, as individuals, we have the power to choose how we let anger control us.
3. Share with the girls that the best way to correct an unhealthy behavior is to assess the behavior and then develop other healthy, more productive alternatives to the unhealthy behavior.
4. Introduce and distribute the **Anger Assessment** handout.
5. Read the opening caption and explain the directions.
6. Permit those girls who would like to share an opportunity to do so.
7. In conclusion, read over and distribute the **Anger's Course** handout.
8. Always end the activity with the Five Star Girl Pledge.

Materials Needed:
1. **Anger Assessment** handout
2. **Anger's Course** handout
3. Pens or pencils

Anger Assessment

Everybody gets angry…sometimes. And this is so because anger is a normal human emotion that can have its way with the best of us on the wrong day. Our challenge, therefore, is not to lie to ourselves and say that we never get angry; or justify our anger fits by saying that there's nothing we can do to control them. Rather, we must get to a place where we are honest enough and mature enough to keep anger and those things that cause us to become angry in perspective—remembering that it is never about anyone else more than it is about self. This Anger Assessment Form is a tool to help evaluate your anger as well as come up with healthy alternatives to becoming angry.

I Get Angry When	I Get Angry Because	Instead of Getting Angry I Could
Example: *My mother fusses at me.*	*She shouldn't talk to be like that.*	*Ignore her. Pray while she's fussing.*
I am left out and not included.	*I want to be liked and accepted.*	*Find people who like me for me.*
______________	______________	______________
______________	______________	______________
______________	______________	______________
______________	______________	______________
______________	______________	______________
______________	______________	______________

Module 6 Activity 2 Handout

Anger's Course

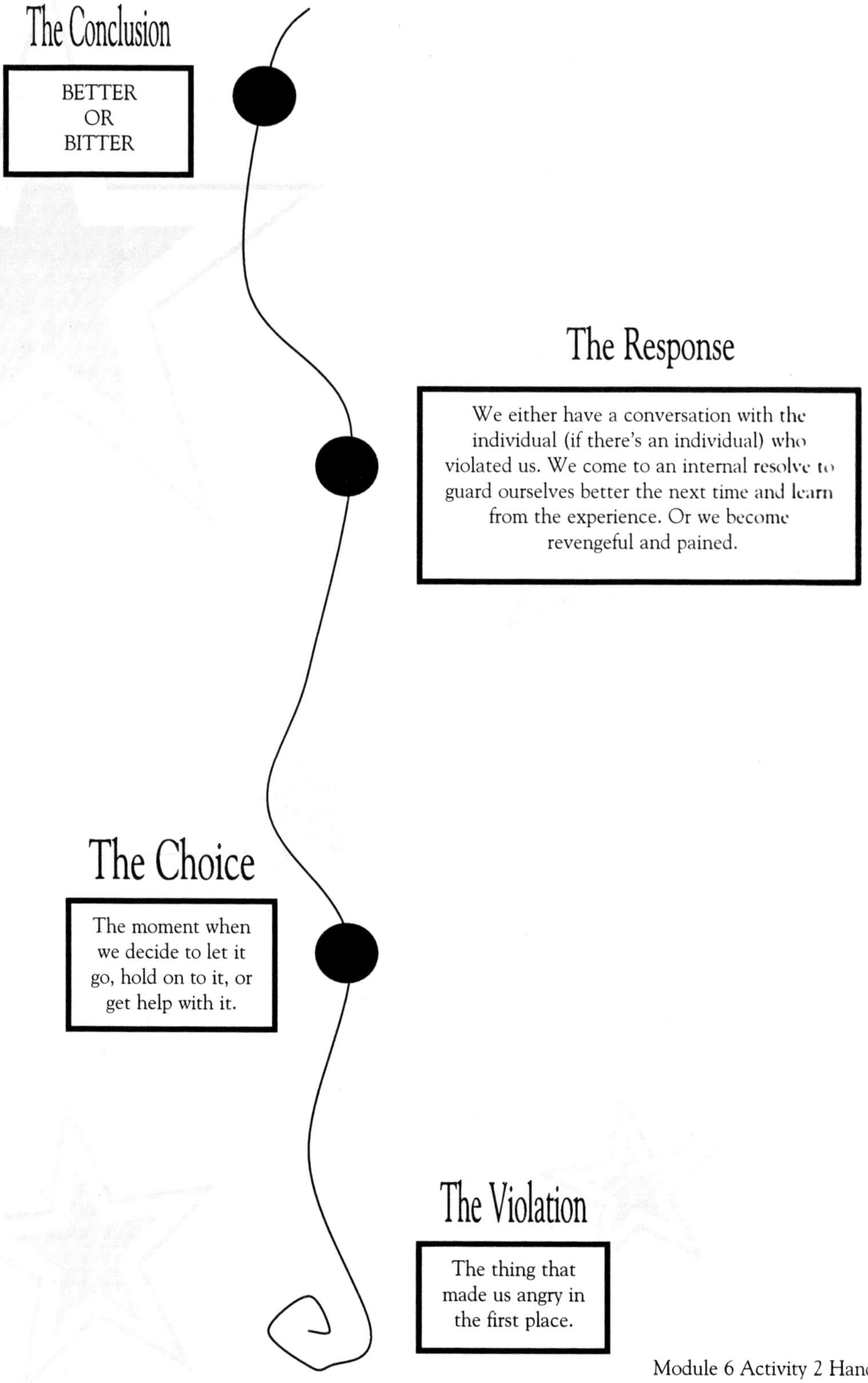

Module 6 Activity 2 Handout

Module Seven: I Choose to Forgive

Five Star Girl Quote:
"As long as you can find someone else to blame for anything you are doing, you cannot be held accountable or responsible for your growth or the lack of it."
Sun Bear

Module Goals:

1. To introduce reasons why forgiving is so difficult.
2. To demonstrate how growth is stagnated by unforgiveness.
3. To share the benefits of forgiving.

Module Overview:

Whether the challenge is to forgive ourselves or someone else, it ought not be a matter of if, but when we will forgive. For opting not to forgive virtually blocks our pathway to happiness, fulfillment and peace. Opting not to forgive essentially imprisons us to that thing or that pain we claim we want to get far away from. Ultimately, though, opting not to forgive diminishes our quality of life and prevents us from enjoying an existence not dictated to by pain.

It is said that there are two main reasons why most of us do not forgive: 1.) We do not know how to forgive, and 2.) We often feel as though the person that we need to extend forgiveness to is somehow unworthy or undeserving of our forgiveness. As authentic as these two reasons may be, we must (even if it takes the help of coaching or counseling) grow to a place where our maturity means we will be more responsible with ourselves as well as to others when it comes to the matter of forgiveness. Also, despite the difficulties we face with extending forgiveness, it will be our understanding of how beneficial forgiveness is to us on a social, spiritual, mental and emotional level that will inevitably cause us to freely choose to forgive.

When we talk about forgiveness, it is important to note that forgiving is different for females than it is for males. Although females are more likely to forgive than males, females, interestingly enough, tend to be choosy about who they will forgive and the extent to which they will forgive. Research gives us to know that females quickly and are more likely to forgive those of the opposite sex than they are to forgive those of the same sex—particularly if the other female is not a family member. It is also noted that females, unlike males, will render forgiveness more times to the same person. However, once a female has reached her limit, and has heard all of the apologizes she can stand, that perpetual offender is written off with almost no chance of return. What is important for girls to know, therefore, is how our inability to forgive one another divides us and causes us to not see our true need for each other. Choosing to forgive, however, joins us together and places us on the same side.

Module Activities:

1. Forgiveness & Me
2. It's Never Too Late
3. Poetically Speaking

Fact Finding:

- We are more likely to forgive acts of violence committed by one of our own group than by someone with whom we did not associate. Ed Cairns, Ph.D., at the University of Ulster, Northern Ireland in the Centre for the Study of Conflict,

ACTIVITY 1: FORGIVENESS & ME

Activity Purpose:
The purpose of this activity is to look at why forgiving is so difficult.

Directions:
After a brief discussion about forgiveness each girl will be given a **Forgiveness & Me** handout to be completed based upon their own personal experiences.

Instructional Procedures:
1. Open with reciting the Five Star Girl Pledge.
2. Begin the session with a dialogue about forgiveness—why others choose not to forgive, what makes forgiving difficult for us, and how deciding to forgive makes us feel.
3. Ask the girls to voluntarily and briefly share one reason why they believe forgiveness is so challenging for most people.
4. Introduce and distribute the **Forgiveness & Me** handout.
5. Read the opening caption and explain the directions.
6. Permit those girls who would like to share an opportunity to do so.
7. Always end the activity with the Five Star Girl Pledge.

Materials Needed:
1. **Forgiveness & Me** handout
2. Pens or pencils

Forgiveness & Me

Nobody wins when we simply pretend. We go through the motions but still operate with the notion that we are free when we really are living in misery. Take a few moments to evaluate your thoughts about forgiveness to see if you are really free or just walking around in misery.

I think that people don't forgive because . . .

1. ______________________________
2. ______________________________
3. ______________________________
4. ______________________________
5. ______________________________

I find forgiving difficult because . . .

1. ______________________________
2. ______________________________
3. ______________________________
4. ______________________________
5. ______________________________

When I do finally forgive, I feel . . .

1. ______________________________
2. ______________________________
3. ______________________________
4. ______________________________
5. ______________________________

Module 7 Activity 1 Handout

ACTIVITY 2: IT'S NEVER TOO LATE

Activity Purpose:

The purpose of this activity is to have girls experience the freedom and the power of forgiving.

Directions:

After listening to Yolanda Adams' song titled **"Never Give Up"** from the Believe CD, girls are asked to answer questions derived from the song's lyrics.

Instructional Procedures:

1. Open with reciting the Five Star Girl Pledge.
2. Revisit the matter of forgiveness. Talk about how not forgiving can create discomfort and friction internally. Discuss how it can make us feel so bad about ourselves that we will use ourselves against ourselves. (Explain this dynamic of self crucifixion.)
3. Ask the girls to share a time when they needed to forgive themselves but didn't feel worthy of forgiveness. Or a time when they needed to be forgiven and the person who needed to forgive them was reluctant to do so.
4. Play Yolanda Adams' **"Never Give Up"** song. (Play time 5:17)
5. Following the song, introduce and distribute the **It's Never Too Late** handout.
6. Read the opening caption and explain the directions.
7. Permit those girls who would like to share an opportunity to do so.
8. Always end the activity with the Five Star Girl Pledge.

Materials Needed:

1. CD Player
2. Yolanda Adams' Believe CD
3. **It's Never Too Late** handout
4. Pens or pencils

It's Never Too Late

There are a lot of people walking around in the world unhappy, unfocused, and unable to reach their maximum potential because they allow themselves to be held hostage by their refusal to forgive. And the hurt that they think they are inflicting upon the person they refuse to forgive is actually hurt they are inflicting upon themselves. In Yolanda Adams' "Never Give Up" song she says a number of things relevant to moving on and overcoming obstacles. Having listened to this song, answer the following questions that correspond to the following lyrics.

Lyric: *"You need courage if you're gonna persevere."*

Question: What part does courage play in forgiving? And how does forgiving help you to persevere?

Lyric: *"Keep the dream alive, don't let it die."*

Question: In what way can unforgiveness kill our dreams?

Lyric: *"Sometimes life can place a stumbling block in your way..."*

Question: When does failing to forgive become a stumbling block?

Lyric: *"It's all inside of you – you have everything you need."*

Question: What is the "everything" you need that's already inside of you when it comes to being able to forgive someone?

Lyric: *"Bring what's deep inside your heart to the light."*

Question: When you forgive, how do you bring what's deep inside your heart to the light?

Lyric: *"Every victory comes in time, work today to change tomorrow."*

Question: How does forgiving someone today bring victory that will change your tomorrow?

Module 7 Activity 2 Handout

ACTIVITY 3: POETICALLY SPEAKING

Activity Purpose:

The purpose of this activity is to have girls look at the domino affect of unforgiveness and its capacity to damage people and relationships.

Directions:

The facilitator will read a poem entitled "Generational Misery" to the girls and have them discuss/dissect its meaning.

Instructional Procedures:

1. Open with reciting the Five Star Girl Pledge.
2. Begin the session with continuing to deal with the matter of forgiveness.
3. Share with the girls that you will be reading a poem entitled **"Generational Misery,"** and once you are done you would like for them to discuss/dissect it.
4. The girls will then be asked to express their feelings about forgiveness by likewise writing a poem of their own.
5. Distribute writing paper and pens/pencils.
6. Permit those girls who would like to share an opportunity to do so.
7. Always end the activity with the Five Star Girl Pledge.

Materials Needed:

1. "Generational Misery" poem
2. Paper
3. Pens or pencils

Generational Misery

This rivalry is killing me.
I look at you and me is who I see.
It's then that I become afraid—
afraid that you'll make
some of the same mistakes I made.
Afraid that men will rule your life,
make you all kinds of empty promises
and before you know it he has a wife—
and it isn't even you.
It happened to me . . . and there I was about to drown in a ses pool of misery.

I look at you and me is who I see.
The me I wanted to be,
but she slipped away.
I would look in the mirror
and everyday I vowed
to put me first,
yet over the years the bad thoughts
only became increasingly worse.

I look at you and me is who I see.
My mother said to me
the same evil things I say to you . . .
and believe it or not that's exactly what I swore I wouldn't do.
I told myself me and my daughter would
be the best of friends.
I said I'd candidly school you about love, sex and men.
I promised I'd allow you to voice your feelings
without going off the deep end.
I pledged that I'd never do anything so painful
that we couldn't come together
and make a m e n d s.

But somehow . . . somehow I messed up. Now we're in the same r u t.
Our relationship too is s t r a i n e d and sour.
I get angry and ashamed as I look at myself and realize I gave away my power.
I didn't know this stuff was embedded in me so deep
that the very thing I despised about my mother I now r e p e a t.

You may not understand, but this place I'm in scares me . . .
particularly because when I look at you me is who I see.

Module 7 Activity 3 Handout

Generational Misery continued

And sweetheart my problem is I don't want you to be me.
I'm a woman who's been emotionally malnourished
and affectionately deprived since I was a young girl.
I'm from a world where nobody affirmed me.
Now humiliatingly, I admit
I am unable to affirm you . . .
and hold you . . .
and love you like a mother should.
I would if . . .
I could if . . .
I had the courage to
but I don't know how or what to do.
It pains me that I don't have a clue
how to resolve my present irreconcilably issues.
It's disenchanting to think that this hasn't been about you
yet I made you believe it was.
I performed like I really had a cause
for mistreating you.

Now . . . now I know this rivalry has been about me,
and it's unfortunate that it took all these years for me to see
that the projection of my misery
has become your stronghold.
The demon of my dysfunction has been
visited upon y o u.
I l o o k . . . I s e e . . . but I don't know what to do.
Because how can I call out in you
what's still very much alive in me—
e s p e c i a l l y if I still struggle with deserving to be free.

This demon tells me it has a r i g h t to exist
because to kill it I must also kill a part of my mother,
and nobody wants their mother to die.
How do I say good-bye
to my mother?
All this time I thought I was to accept her anyway she comes
because I don't get another one . . .

But baby girl that's a lie.
Every thing that's evil has it's appointed time to die.
You deserve better and so do I.
From the depths of my soul
I ask God to deliver us both from this stronghold.

Module 7 Activity 3 Handout

Generational Misery continued

I pray that He'd tear down our towers of pain
and reconstruct our lives with resurrecting change.
I pray that there will be no residual agony
that clouds your heart and prevents you from
trusting or accepting me . . .
Yes. I'm aware that this process isn't going to be easy—
and sweetheart I'm okay with that.
I can't dare expect you to be where I'm at.
It took me all these years to get here.
Yet . . . Yet I would be remiss if I didn't encourage you
to not wallow in unforgiveness too long . . .
Staying there won't erase the wrong,
and as I've found you only end up doing
yourself a lot of harm.

Somehow . . . Some way . . . Someday . . .
I pray you can forgive me
for placing you on the frontline of an
u n n e c e s s a r y rivalry.

Module Eight: Friendships & Relationships

Five Star Girl Quote:
"People come into your life for a reason, a season or a lifetime. When you figure out which it is, you know exactly what to do."
Michelle Ventor

Module Goals:

1. To help girls identify the difference between a healthy and an unhealthy friendship or relationship.
2. To convey to girls that not accepting someone as your friend can sometimes be a necessary course of action.

Module Overview:

"We need to rid ourselves of the fiction that girls should like and be friends with everyone. Encourage girls to choose people as friends who are affirming, who listen to them and treat them well. It's okay not to be friends with someone as long as you treat that person respectfully. Most important, mistreatment is not a quality of friendship," says Lyn Mikel Brown, Ed.D.

Girls place a lot of emphasis and value on friendships and relationships. Girls value their peers as well as their peers' opinions; because of this there exists a need to always make certain that friendships or relationships are present—even if it means compromising themselves or their core convictions. Crucial to the safety and well being of girls is the need to develop standards and boundaries that dictate the parameters of acceptable relationships. No longer can girls think that they must have relationships by any means necessary. In addition to helping girls develop standards and boundaries is a need to teach girls how to rebound when someone fails to honor or respect the standards and boundaries set forth.

Paramount in all of this is the underlining issue of respect. Girls must know that others will only respect them to the degree they respect themselves. For respecting one's self begins with a vow and a practice to not stay with or around unhealthy people. Respecting one's self ultimately demands that we demand the best for ourselves—regardless of how lonely it may feel.

Module Activities:

1. Treat Her Like a Lady
2. The Measuring stick of Friendship
3. Healthy vs. Unhealthy Relationships

Fact Finding:

- **There is a movement within feminism that believes the female orientation to relationship and connection—to nurturing and caregiving—gives women a uniquely wise approach to the their world. Popularity, however, turns this phenomenon on its head. In the race to be cool, some girls transform friendship into a series of deals and calculations, using relationship as much to destroy as to build. Relationship is no longer simply an end; it is also a means. Rachel Simmons, Author of *Odd Girl Out***

Activity 1: Treat Her Like A Lady

Activity Purpose:

The purpose of this activity is to have give consideration to how they desire to be treated versus how they currently are allowing themselves to be treated in their respective relationship.

Directions:

After listening to Celine Deon's song titled **"Treat Her Like a Lady"** from the Let's Talk About Love CD, girls are asked to answer questions derived from the song's lyrics.

Instructional Procedures:

1. Open with reciting the Five Star Girl Pledge.
2. Begin the session with a discussion about relationships and why it's important that our goal must be to only find ourselves in healthy, non-threatening relationships.
3. Talk about how easy it is to settle for or accept what you know you don't deserve if you aren't careful.
4. Inform the girls that you all are about to listen to Celine Dion's "**Treat Her Like a Lady"** and that following the song you will distribute a handout with questions for them to answer.
5. Play **"Treat Her Like a Lady"**.
6. Following the song distribute the **Treat Her Like a Lady** handout, allow approximately 15 minutes for them to answer the questions, and then permit those girls who would like to share an opportunity to do so.
7. Always end the activity with the Five Star Girl Pledge.

Materials Needed:

1. CD Player
2. Celine Deon's **Let's Talk About Love** CD
3. **Treat Her Like a Lady** handout
4. Pens or pencils

Treat Her Like A Lady

After listening to Celine Dion's **"Treat Her Like a Lady"**, answer the following questions.

Lyric: *"All the girl could want was a little attention . . . But all that boy wants is to hit and run off..."*

Question: Why do you think girls and guys are often seeking to get different things from the same relationship?

Lyric: *"He and his friends – they sit and they laugh going around talking 'bout the girls they used in the past."*

Question: What type of guys use girls and sit around with their boys to laugh about it?

Lyric: *"You'll make a good girl crazy if you don't treat her like a lady."*

Question: How can a guy make a girl go crazy by not treating her like a lady?

Lyric: *"She stopped going to church, she don't wanna go to school. She left with anger when he took her for a fool, even though her friends tell her to just keep cool. Didn't tell her from the start just what he had planned. Right in her face with another woman. Now she's in jail for attacking her man."*

Question: Do you think you would allow yourself to get to this point in a relationship, or would you leave first?

Lyric: *"You're gonna get what's coming to you for all the bad things you do to your lady."*

Question: Have you ever treated a guy bad in a relationship and it came back to you? Or has a guy treated you bad in a relationship and it came back to him?

Lyric: "*Tell it to her straight, she can take the truth. Don't lead her on and leave her confused. Anyone would rather be alone than be used. Don't sit and think you'll hurt her feelings. She only wants to know just what the deal is. Next time beware of who's heart your breaking (or stealing)"*

Question: Why do you think many people choose to lie or be deceitful in relationships, rather than tell the truth?

ACTIVITY 2: THE MEASURING STICK OF FRIENDSHIP

Activity Purpose:

The purpose of this activity is to have girls develop a simple yet accurate way to determine if they are in safe friendships.

Directions:

Girls will use the **How Does Your Friends Measure Up?** measuring stick to identify the characteristics of those they call friend.

Instructional Procedures:

1. Open with reciting the Five Star Girl Pledge.
2. Begin the session with a discussion about friendships and why we must choose our friends wisely; not based upon the things they have on the outside, but based upon what they are made of on the inside.
3. Ask the girls how they typical choose their friends. Ask the girls if any of them have friends that they are not happy with, or feel they should get rid of. Share with the girls that periodically we have to take a look at the people we call "friend" to see if they really are friends or just dead weight.
4. Distribute the **How Does Your Friends Measure Up?** handout, allow approximately 15 minutes for the girls to complete the handout. Then permit those girls who would like to share an opportunity to do so.
5. Always end the activity with the Five Star Girl Pledge.

Materials Needed:

1. **How Does Your Friends Measure Up?** handout
2. Pens or pencils

How Does Your Friends Measure Up?

Spend a few moments assessing the friends you have and where they would fall on the measuring stick of friendship. Write your friends' names next to as many characteristics that apply to him/her.

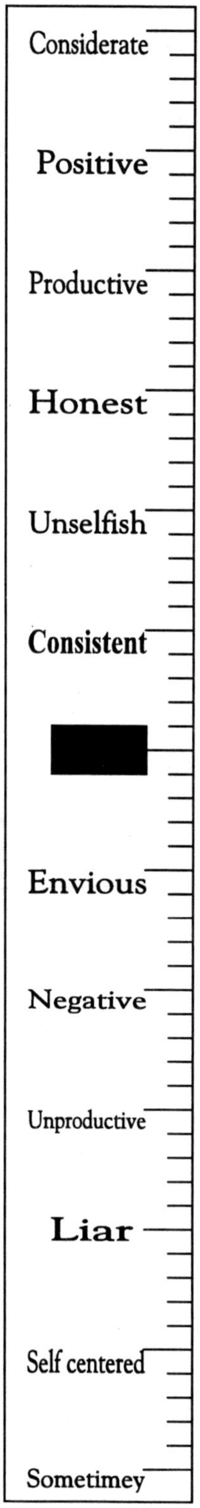

Module 8 Activity 2 Handout

ACTIVITY 3: HEALTHY VS. UNHEALTHY RELATIONSHIPS

Activity Purpose:

The purpose of this activity is to educate girls about the white flags of a healthy relationship and the red flags of an unhealthy relationship.

Directions:

The girls read about to the Kemba Smith story; a story about a young lady who ended up in an unhealthy relationship, served time in prison, but in the end was pardoned by former President Bill Clinton, and is *now* living a victorious life championing the cause against mandatory sentencing for first-time, non-violent offenders. Following the reading, girls will share their thoughts by answering questions from the **Kemba Smith Story** facilitator's handout. Finally, the girls will demonstrate their learned knowledge of healthy/unhealthy relationships by doing the **White Flag, Red Flag** handout.

Instructional Procedures:

1. Open with reciting the Five Star Girl Pledge.
2. Begin the session with a discussion about relationships and how we must keep our finger on the pulse of our relationships by assessing them periodically.
3. Ask the girls when was the last time they really stopped to check on how things were going…feeling…progressing, etc.
4. Share with the girls that often times people in relationships begin to take each other for granted because they've stopped checking in to see how things are going, and what ends up happening is people will assume everything is okay when in fact it may not be at all.
5. Move on to discuss and explore the Kemba Smith story. Go to http://www.drcnet.org/rapid/1997/9-12-1.html#kemba and print out a copy of the story. Also go to your local library to locate the April 1996 Emerge Magazine issue featuring the Kemba's Nightmare story. Make enough copies of the article for each girl to have and read. Discuss the Kemba Smith story in depth. Then have the girls answer the questions on the Kemba Smith Story facilitator's handout.

6. Following your discussion, distribute the **White Flag, Red Flag** handout along with the **White Flag, Red Flag Corresponding Statements** handout. Allow approximately 10 minutes for the girls to complete the handout, and then permit those girls who would like to share an opportunity to do so.
7. Always end the activity with the Five Star Girl Pledge.

Materials Needed:

1. April 1996 Emerge Magazine Issue
2. **White Flag, Red Flag** handout
3. **White Flag, Red Flag Corresponding Statements** handout
4. **Kemba Smith Story** facilitator handout
5. Pens or pencils

Kemba Smith Story

After having read the Kemba Smith story with and to the participants, create a discussion using the following questions.

1. Who is Kemba Smith?
2. What has happened in her life in the article?
3. What do you think made Kemba get involved with a drug dealer?
4. Why do you think Kemba stayed in the relationship after she found out what her boyfriend was about?
5. Do you feel that Kemba should have been arrested?
6. Why do you think Kemba didn't get help or tell somebody what she knew?
7. What, in your opinion, causes a girl, like in Kemba's case, to allow a guy to fully control her?
8. Were there any red flags that Kemba missed?
9. With all that Kemba had going for her—a loving two parent family, raised in a nice neighborhood, intelligence, never been in trouble before—what do you think caused her to stray from her foundation and her core values?
10. What is the lesson *you* take from the Kemba Smith story?

Module 8 Activity 3 Handout

White Flag, Red Flag

Take the statements from the corresponding handout and tape or glue them in the either a white flag or a red flag. (The red flag is actually grey.)

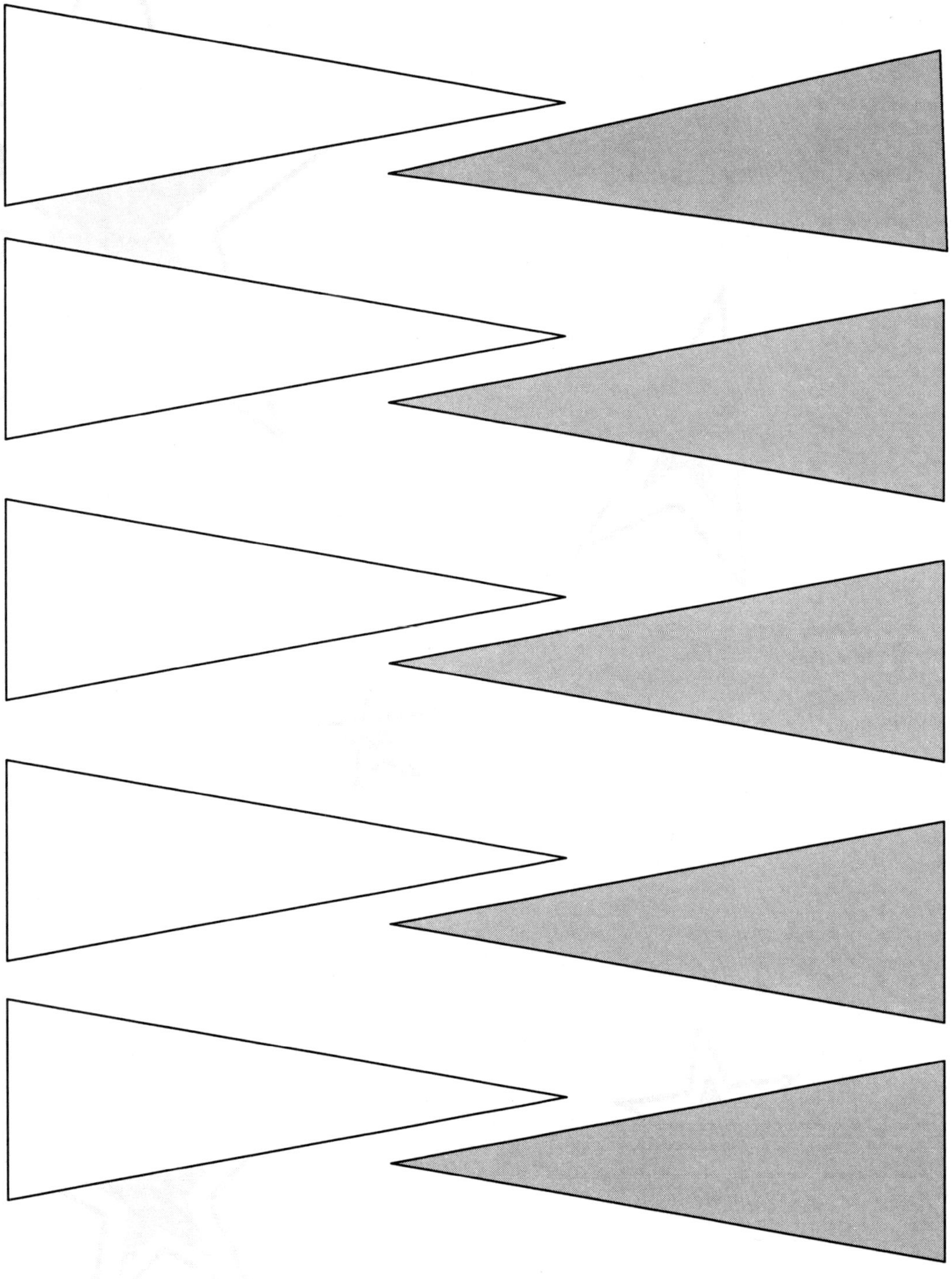

Module 8 Activity 3 Handout

White Flag, Red Flag
Corresponding Statements

Cut the following statements out and tape or glue them in either a white flag or a red flag based upon where you think they should go.

1.
He sees other girls and
doesn't care if you know.

2.
All the two of you do is fuss.

3.
He's always kind
and gentlemen-like.

4.
He calls you out
of your name.

5.
He likes doing
nice things for you.

6.
You never go anywhere.

7.
He does what he
says he's going to do.

8.
He calls you
endearing nick names.

9.
You've lost respect
for each other.

10.
He speaks well
of his mother.

Module 8 Activity 3 Handout

ACTIVITY 4: GIRLFRIENDS

Activity Purpose:

The purpose of this activity is to encourage girls to have more respectful and trusting friendships with one another.

Directions:

Girls will be paired in groups of two and asked to sit for 2 minutes simply looking at one another. Following the 2 minutes, the facilitator will point to a paired set of girls at which time each girl will be asked to say as many nice things as they can about the girl they are partnered with.

Instructional Procedures:

1. Open with reciting the Five Star Girl Pledge.
2. Begin the session with a discussion about girls and women, and how it's often said that we have a difficult time being real, true friends to each other because we are so catey, phony, and backstabbing.
3. Instruct the girls to pair off in groups of two.
4. Tell the girls that their charge is to spend the next 2 minutes looking at one another very carefully.
5. Explain to the girls that at the conclusion of the 2 minutes they must say as many nice things about their partner as they can.
6. Before concluding, ask the girls how it felt to stare at another girl for 2 minutes, and also how it felt to only be able to say nice things.
7. Always end the activity with the Five Star Girl Pledge.

Materials Needed:

1. Open, honest minds

Module Nine:
Family Dynamics

Five Star Girl Quote:
"At our best level of existence we are parts of a family, and at our highest level of achievement we work to keep the family alive."
Maya Angelou

Module Goals:

1. To help girls come to terms with our new day "family."
2. To provide a healthy outlet for girls to deal with the familial changes they cannot control yet have to live within.
3. To make parents aware of girls' feelings around the whole matter of family dynamics.

Module Overview:

It is no secret that today's family, in many instances, is not what it used to be. Now more than ever, the traditional family (a mother, a father, and children born of that same mother and father all living under the same roof) is becoming a thing of the past. In a society with a fifty percent and climbing divorce rate, single families and blended families are our new norm. What this dynamic means for girls, in particular, is an increase in responsibility that can range from helping to tend to her younger siblings to a part-time job to help make ends meet to living in a home with a man or perhaps an older stepbrother that she hardly knows and is skeptical about thus a more strained relationship with her biological parent. Such family dynamics are increasingly affecting girls in their physical development as well as in their mental development, yet it has a sometimes adverse affect on their emotional development.

"Childhood stress may be one of the culprits behind an alarming phenomenon: girls reaching puberty at an early age," reports Amanda Dunn. "Emotionally too, puberty takes its toll." The Director of the Centre for Adolescent Health, Professor George Patton, says studies have shown a link between early puberty and depression. We, therefore, must wrap girls in a support system that is conducive to protecting their youth even as they live in environments that threaten it. Needed also is parents' awareness of how change, too much responsibility too soon, and not enough affirmation and attention weighs on their daughters sense of self. Too often parents will place girls in a position to undertake adult-like responsibility but then fail to understand why their daughter is "so grown . . . so fast . . . so beyond her age."

Module Activities:

1. Vignette: Who Do I Tell?
2. Outsider
3. Confession Is Good for the Soul

Fact Finding:

- **Julie Quinklivan, a research director from Melbourne's Royal Women's Hospital, interviewed 100 pregnant women, half aged under 20. Of those who began menstruating earlier, Dr. Quinlivan found that 37 percent had been exposed to violence and 57 percent to parental divorce.**

ACTIVITY 1: VIGNETTE: WHO DO I TELL?

Activity Purpose:

The purpose of this activity is to teach girls how to approach delicate family matters.

Directions:

After listening to a vignette, girls will discuss different approaches to resolving family conflicts.

Instructional Procedures:

1. Open with reciting the Five Star Girl Pledge.
2. Begin the session with a discussion about family; how it has changed over the years; how there are a lot more single family homes; how parents are so busy working that sometimes children feel left out or ignored.
3. Let the girls know that you are going to read the **Vignette: Who Do I Tell?** and after you've read the vignette you all will discuss the different dynamics of the family conflict as well as the best approaches to resolving the conflict. Use the questions below the vignette to guide your discussion.
4. Always end the activity with the Five Star Girl Pledge.

Materials Needed:

1. **Vignette: Who Do I Tell?** handout

Vignette: Who Do I Tell?

Sarah is the 13 year old middle child in a family of five. Originally it was her two little brothers, her mother and herself. About six months ago Sarah's mother remarried. Now it's her two little brothers, her mother, her stepfather and her stepfather's two older sons who are 15 and 18 years old. Since the two families have merged and moved in together Sarah has noticed that her 18 year old stepbrother keeps looking at her strange, as if he wants her or something. To avoid his looks Sarah tries to stay as far away from him as possible. One night while Sarah was lying across her bed doing her homework, the 18 year old stood in Sarah's door gazing at her with an annoying smirk on his face. Once Sarah noticed him, she got up and closed her door.

Because Sarah really likes her stepfather; because Sarah doesn't want to trouble her mother at a time when she is so happy, Sarah contemplates whether or not she should say something as well as who she could even say something to.

Questions:

1. Is Sarah's imagination getting the best of her?

2. Will her mother believe her, or will she think that Sarah is just not handling the merging of the two families well?

3. If Sarah talked to her stepfather would he hear her or immediately take his son's side?

4. Could it be possible that Sarah is the one who wants her stepbrother and is deliberately drawing attention to herself?

5. Why would an 18 year old be after his 13 year old stepsister?

6. Would it make sense for Sarah to discuss her concerns openly at the dinner table or should she pull her mother and stepfather together privately?

7. Might Sarah's 18 year old stepbrother listen to her if she tried to confront him herself?

8. If you were Sarah, what would you do?

Module 9 Activity 1 Handout

ACTIVITY 2: OUTSIDER

Activity Purpose:

The purpose of this activity is to have girls put in perspective the moments of isolation and alienation we can sometimes experience right in our own homes with our own family members.

Directions:

After listening to Mariah Carey' song titled **"Outsider"** from the Butterfly CD, girls are asked to answer questions derived from the song's lyrics.

Instructional Procedures:

1. Open with reciting the Five Star Girl Pledge.
2. Begin the session with a dialogue about how because we are individuals with different minds and different dreams, we can sometimes feel out of place in our family; as if we don't belong.
3. Ask the girls to briefly talk about a moment when or if they felt like an outsider in their family.
4. Let the girls know that you all are going to listen to Maria Carey's song titled ***"Outsider"***.
5. Play Mariah Carey' ***"Outsider"*** song. (Play time 5:17)
6. Following the song, introduce and distribute the **Outsider** handout.
7. Read the opening caption and explain the directions.
8. Permit those girls who would like to share an opportunity to do so.
9. Always end the activity with the Five Star Girl Pledge.

Materials Needed:

1. CD Player
2. Mariah Carey' Butterfly CD
3. **Outsider** handout
4. Pens or pencils

Outsider

You have just listened to Mariah Carey's Outsider, now read through the lyrics and answer the following questions associated with the lyrics.

Question:

1. What is the "strange" that Mariah Carey is talking about?

2. What are the lyrics *"standing alone eager to just believe it's good enough to be what you really are but in your heart uncertainty forever lies and you'll always be somewhere on the outside"* saying?

3. At what point do you think most girls begin to experience *"the realization that you don't have a space where you fit in and recognize you where born to exist"*, and why do you think these feelings arise?

4. What would you say is most *"hard"* about feeling like an outsider?

5. Why does Mariah Carey compare being an outsider to that of being "*blind and unguided into a world divided"?*

6. Based upon the lyrics, *"You're thrown where you're never quite the same although you try—try and try to tell yourself you really are,"* why do some people choose to stay in denial about how alone they feel?

7. What, if anything else, stuck out for you in the song?

Activity 3: Confession Is Good for the Soul

Activity Purpose:

The purpose of this activity is to have girls divulge their feelings about their family unit.

Directions:

Girls will write a letter to their parents/caregiver either to respectfully divulge those things that they find troubling or unsettling when it comes to their family setting; or to express how good it feels to be in a family where they feel loved and appreciated.

Instructional Procedures:

1. Open with reciting the Five Star Girl Pledge.
2. Begin the session by reiterating your discussion about family. Share with the girls the importance of being able to freely express their feelings—within the confines of their family unit.
3. Gauge from the girls their comfort or discomfort with communicating with their parents/caregivers.
4. Tell the girls that their assignment is to write a one page letter to their parents/caregiver to either respectfully divulge those things that they find troubling or unsettling when it comes to their family; or to express how good it feels to be in a family where they feel loved and appreciated.
5. Give the girls approximately 30 minutes to draft their letters. While they are writing, walk around the room to see if there are any questions or challenges.
6. Always end the activity with the Five Star Girl Pledge.

Materials Needed:

1. Writing paper
2. Pens

MODULE TEN: THE FATHER FACTOR

Five Star Girl Quote: "Take a day to heal from the lies you've told yourself and the ones that have been told to you." Maya Angelou

MODULE GOALS:

1. To encourage the hearts of girls who may be struggling with the absence of their father.
2. To present a look at how girls are affected—mentally, socially, academically and behaviorally by their father's absence.

MODULE OVERVIEW:

As a society, we often talk about how much boys need their fathers. We are quick to point out the devastating effects of men not being in their sons' lives. The fact of the matter is like boys, girls are suffering at alarming rates and on many levels as a result of not having a father in whom they can depend upon as well. As purported by Lohr, Leg, Mendell and Reimer in their study, "Girls with absent fathers grow up without the day-by-day experience of attentive, caring and loving interaction with a man. Without this continuous sense of being valued and loved, a young girl does not thrive, but rather is stunted in her emotional development."

To effectively and wholistically serve our girls, we must be real clear about their need for a father's presence in their lives. We must listen to our girls and create a healthy platform for them to articulate the pain and/or the disappointment they contend with because their father is not around. We must also talk with mothers to ensure that they are not deliberately creating barriers for their daughter to have access to her father. Finally, we must find absent and neglectful fathers and educate them about how absolutely necessary their presence is with respect to the healthy development of their daughter.

As clinicians and practitioners, parents and teachers, we have to develop a level of sensitivity to the behavior we see our girls displaying and its correlation to the fact that they perhaps are hungering and thirsting for a responsible, loving, caring man to wrap them safely in his love—and for no other reason than he is the father who helped to create her.

MODULE ACTIVITIES:

1. Self Esteem Autobiography
2. Timeline
3. Where Are the Fathers?

FACT FINDING:

- **Fatherless daughters compared to those with present father figures are in higher risk of teenage pregnancy, college dropout and low self esteem. Franklin B. Krohn, SUNY College at Fredonia**

- **Girls who have little contact with their fathers, especially during adolescence had great difficulties forming lasting relationships with men. (Grimm-Wassil, 1994)**

ACTIVITY 1: SELF ESTEEM BIOGRAPHY

Activity Purpose:

The purpose of this activity is to allow the girls to assess the level of their father's influence and/or involvement in their lives.

Directions:

The girls will complete the statements on the **Self Esteem Biography** handout and grade their fathers accordingly.

Instructional Procedures:

1. Open with reciting the "Five Star Girl" Pledge.
2. Begin the session with a dialogue about the difference between mothers and mothers. Talk about the distinction in their roles, and how we need the deposits of both parents in our lives to give us a balanced and wholesome developmental process.
3. Discuss, briefly, the difference statistics offer between girls who have fathers in their lives versus girls who do not. Ask the girls if they can see themselves in any of the data. Spend some time putting it all in perspective.
4. Introduce and distribute the **Self Esteem Biography** handout.
5. Once everyone has finished, allow those girls who would like to share an opportunity to do so.
6. Always end the activity with the "Five Star Girl" Pledge.

Materials Needed:

1. **Self Esteem Biography** handout
2. Pens or pencils

SELF-ESTEEM AUTOBIOGRAPHY

My father helped me ____

____

My father hurt me by ____

____

My father taught me____

____

My father is responsible for ____

____

The best thing my father could do for me now is ______________________

____

If I were to give my father a grade for assisting me with my growth he would he would receive:

__________. Explain the reason(s) for the grade ______________________

____

Grading System

A = Excellent; helped me every step of the way

B = Great job as a parent

C = Good job; helped me with some things in my life

D = Made some attempts to help me

F = Failing; not in my life

"Children are the Reward of Life"
African Proverb

Module 10 Activity 1 Handout

ACTIVITY 2: TIMELINE

Activity Purpose:

The purpose of this activity is for girls to chart out their lives—with or without the presence of their father—so as to see how their lives have progressed and are continuing to progress.

Directions:

The girls will create a timeline based on their life. The timeline serves as a biography of things that have occurred in their life in sequential order.

Instructional Procedures:

1. Open with reciting the Five Star Girl Pledge.
2. Begin this activity by talking about the fact that each of us, as we breath and live, are daily experiencing things that shape who we are and impact the way we see the world.
3. Share with the girls that for this activity they will be looking at the progression of their lives by doing a timeline.
4. As the facilitator, you will distribute an example of what a timeline would look like. It is important that the facilitator realizes that youth people are looking to connect with adults. Often the connections can be made based on opening up the dialogue around issues which have impacted the facilitator (ex. Death of a loved one, fatal or traumatic accident, etc.).
5. In giving your direction, make sure that the girls understand that their timeline should begin with their year of birth and move to the present. On the top line participants will begin to think about positive memories they have had growing up. These will be indicated along with the age of the event. At the bottom of the time line the participants will list the negative and or traumatic things which have occurred in their life.
6. Once everyone has finished, allow those girls who would like to share an opportunity to do so.
7. Always end the activity with the Five Star Girl Pledge.

Materials Needed:

1. **Timeline** handout
2. Pens or pencils

TIMELINE

Girls will create a timeline based on their life. Although many of the things that have happened to us may be difficult to discuss, these occurrences represent a part of our life. Life is based on the bitter and the sweet. We all have both positive and negative memories from our childhood that are often not discussed. Please begin your timeline by identifying the positive things which have occurred during your childhood (ex. Getting your first bike, graduating from elementary school, hitting the jump shot with a few second left on the clock, getting your nails done for the first time, grabbing the attention of a boy you really liked, etc.)

Positive

Birth	6	9	10	12	15	Present

Negative

The timeline serves as a biography of things that have occurred in your life. The following are a few things to think about as you develop your timeline:

- Relationships with family members
- Positive/negative events that have occurred during childhood (death of a loved one, family member going to prison and or accident)
- Events that happened in the community or school
- Memories of holidays
- Encounters with the police and other law enforcement entities

Module 10 Activity 2 Handout

ACTIVITY 3: WHERE ARE THE FATHERS?

Activity Purpose:

The purpose of this activity is to have girls reflect upon and assess what it's like to have or not have their father in their lives.

Directions:

By participating in a focus group, girls will assess the degree to which having a father or not having a father impacts a girl's life. Please note: there will need to be two facilitators for this activity as two focus groups will be conducted at the same time. The girls who's fathers are **absent** will participate in one focus group, while the girls who's fathers are **active** will simultaneously be participating in another focus group. The focus groups are to be no more than 45 minutes to 1 hour in length. The focus group instructions and questions for both groups are provided on the **Where Are the Fathers?** handouts.

Instructional Procedures:

1. Open with reciting the Five Star Girl Pledge.
2. Begin this activity by reiterating the fact that some girls are fortunate enough to have their father in their life, while other girls are not quite as fortunate. Make certain you spend some time letting the girls know that when a father decides to be absent from his child's life it has nothing at all to do with the child.
3. Move on to discuss some of the reasons why fathers may be absent.
4. Ask by show of hands, who's father is active and who's father is absent.
5. Instruct the girls who's fathers are absent to move to one side of the room, while the girls who's fathers are active are to move to the other side of the room.
6. Share with both groups of girls that they are going to be participating in a focus group, explain what a focus group is, and then further explain what you and the other facilitator hope to learn from these two focus groups in particular. Also, inform the participants that they will receive an incentive gift for their participation in the focus group.
7. Break up into two groups. Once you get settled in your room, have the girls listen to Bishop T. D. Jakes' ***Where Are the Fathers?*** song.
8. After the song, proceed with the instructions on the focus group handout. At the conclusion of the focus group oblige girls who may need to talk privately.
9. Always end the activity with the Five Star Girl Pledge.

Materials Needed:

1. **Where Are the Fathers? Active Dads Focus Group** handout
2. **Where Are the Fathers? Absent Dads Focus Group** handout
3. Bishop T. D. Jakes' He-Motions CD (2 copies)
4. 2 CD players
5. 2 facilitators
6. 2 rooms
7. 2 tape recorders
8. incentive gifts
9. writing pads
10. pens or pencils

WHERE ARE THE FATHERS?
FOCUS GROUP
(ABSENT FATHERS)

As the facilitator, you must present yourself as comfortable as possible so that you can in turn make the participants as comfortable as possible. You are the leader; as such the participants will take their cues from you. To the best of your ability, stay non-bias and non-judgmental. If a participant happens to ask you how you feel about a question, respond by letting her know that for the sake of this focus group your feelings are not relevant, what's important is how they feel.

Before Getting Started:

State the purpose of the focus group. A focus group is a gathering together of a specified group of people to collect data that will help determine the answer to a particular question. For example, when companies are looking to market a new product they will hold a focus group to see if consumers are likely to buy the product. Also, when the state or local government is trying to get a message out via a Public Service Announcement, they will hold a focus group to determine what is the most effective way to present the message to the population they are attempting to target.

State the rules/terms of the focus group. Every participant in this focus group is here voluntarily. At any time you feel like you no longer want to participate you may excuse yourself. However, please know that when you excuse yourself you forfeit the incentive gift that every participant will receive at the conclusion of the focus group. Please be mindful to not cut each other off or talk while someone else is talking.

State what you hope to learn as a result of doing the focus group. Because you all are a very important part of our program; and because we want to provide you with quality and efficient services, we must know what your needs are. We need to know if there are areas of struggle or contention that are prohibiting you from developing into the beautiful, successful women you were created to be. This focus group will help us to determine this—in part. Fathers are a big part of your lives...of your development, and we want to know to what degree is your father influencing or impeding your healthy development. We are going to start by listening to a song titled *"Where Are the Fathers?"* and then I will ask you some questions.

1. What immediately came to mind as you listened to this song?
2. What is the one word you'd use to describe how you feel about your father?
3. Have you ever cried about your father's absence in your life?
4. Do you feel that your father being absent from your life has hurt or helped you?
5. What, in your opinion, would be different if your father were actively involved in your life?
6. Why do you think some men decide to not be involved in their daughters' lives?
7. Is there such a thing as a "good enough" reason for a man walking out on or turning his back on his responsibility as father?
8. Was there a time in your life where you actually said to yourself, *"I wish my father were here?"* If so, when?
9. What do you miss the most about not having your father in your life?
10. How easy or how difficult would it be for you to forgive your father if he asked you to?
11. If your father came through that door right now, what would you do? What would you say to him? Or would you completely ignore him?

WHERE ARE THE FATHERS? FOCUS GROUP (ACTIVE FATHERS)

As the facilitator, you must present yourself as comfortable as possible so that you can in turn make the participants as comfortable as possible. You are the leader; as such the participants will take their cues from you. To the best of your ability, stay non-bias and non-judgmental. If a participant happens to ask you how you feel about a question, respond by letting her know that for the sake of this focus group your feelings are not relevant, what's important is how they feel.

Before Getting Started:

State the purpose of the focus group. A focus group is a gathering together of a specified group of people to collect data that will help determine the answer to a particular question. For example, when companies are looking to market a new product they will hold a focus group to see if consumers are likely to buy the product. Also, when the state or local government is trying to get a message out via a Public Service Announcement, they will hold a focus group to determine what is the most effective way to present the message to the population they are attempting to target.

State the rules/terms of the focus group. Every participant in this focus group is here voluntarily. At any time you feel like you no longer want to participate you may excuse yourself. However, please know that when you excuse yourself you forfeit the incentive gift that every participant will receive at the conclusion of the focus group. Please be mindful to not cut each other off or talk while someone else is talking.

State what you hope to learn as a result of doing the focus group. Because you all are a very important part of our program; and because we want to provide you with quality and efficient services, we must know what your needs are. We need to know if there are areas of struggle or contention that are prohibiting you from developing into the beautiful, successful women you were created to be. This focus group will help us to determine this—in part. Fathers are a big part of your lives...of your development, and we want to know to what degree is your father influencing or impeding your healthy development. We are going to start by listening to a song titled *"Where Are the Fathers?"* and then I will ask you some questions.

1. What immediately came to mind as you listened to this song?
2. What is the one word you'd use to describe how you feel about your father?
3. How has having your father in your life helped you?
4. What, in your opinion, would be different if your father were not actively involved in your life?
5. Why do you think some men decide to not be actively involved in their daughters' lives?
6. In one word, describe how you think girls who don't have fathers in their lives feel?
7. Was there a time in your life where you actually said to yourself, *"I am so thankful I have my dad?"*
   If so, when?
8. Describe your relationship with your father: close, okay, distant, needs work.
9. What do you enjoy the most about having your father in your life?
10. What is the most significant thing your father has taught you to date?

Module 10 Activity 3 Handout

MODULE ELEVEN: RAP, HIP HOP & GIRLS

Five Star Girl Quote:
"Ain't gonna let nobody turn me around..."
African-Amreican Spiritual

MODULE GOALS:

1. To give girls a healthy perspective of their own self image—separate and a part from what music videos depict.
2. To help insulate girls against feeling like they need to succumb to some of rap and hip hop's perception of girls/women.

MODULE OVERVIEW:

All over the country, yea even the world, the buzz is on about rap and hip hop. People are amazed at how it's taking our society by storm. Latinos, Asians, Caucasians, and Africans alike are jumping on the rap and hip hop's band wagon. The love that the African American community has long since had for rap and hip hop is now infiltrating and permeating other races' homes, cars and offices.

Record sales are overwhelmingly high. Corporate America has begun to collaborate with the hip hop industry. Rap and hip hop artists are getting more recognition. But, amidst all of the hype and hoopla are a generation of girls who are wondering how they fit in. They watch and they listen, and can't help but ask themselves: "Is this who I am?" "Is this who I want to be?" "Isn't there more to me than my body?" "Do I have to stoop low to be noticed?" "Why can't they say nicer, more positive things about us as girls?"

Indeed this is not to say that all rap or hip hop is bad or derogatory. It is to say, however, that girls are impacted by that which is. Video after video we see girls with little to nothing on, swirling and grinding, rolling and being made spectacles of. Decency seems to have taken a back seat to the all mighty dollar, and in too many instances it's at the expense of women and girls. To turn this around, we must begin to validate and affirm the worth of girls by letting them know that different is permissible; by telling them that what's in their head is more important than what's underneath their clothing. We have to make every effort to counter the insensitivity of some of our rap and hip hop artists with opportunities to let girls shine by way of their intelligence and the good they do. Finally, we must teach girls that their self image is defined by them not by what is plastered across a TV screen, a billboard, or a magazine page.

MODULE ACTIVITIES:

1. A Journey Into Me
2. Body Image/Self Identity

FACT FINDING:

- **Approximately 75% of the rap and hip hop audience is non-black. Gregory Lewis, The San Francisco Examiner**
- **Today, hip and rip is the fastest growing music genre in the U.S., accounting for more than 10 percent of the 12.3 billion music sales in 1998. Rap music shares of sales has increased 150% over the last ten years and is still rising." Record Industry Association of America**

ACTIVITY 1: A JOURNEY INTO ME

Activity Purpose:

The purpose of this activity is to have girls look at how words create images and images play a role in shaping the heart and minds of girls.

Directions:

As they listen to India Arie's song titled ***"Get It Together"*** from the Voyage to India CD, girls will reflect upon how negative words said to them or about them as females can and do affect what they think of themselves.

Instructional Procedures:

1. Open with reciting the Five Star Girl Pledge.
2. Begin this activity by talking about how at sometime someone has probably told then to "just be yourself". Talk about how this cliché implies two things: that the task is simple and even logical, and that being oneself is enough. Also talk about how if it were as simple as it seems, we would never have to worry about how to act in new situations or question whether the self we presented to others was appropriate.
3. Share with the girls that the way in which an individual perceives herself is of real importance to the character of her behavior. People tend to act as they perceive themselves to be.
4. Let the girls know that you all will be listening to India Arie's song titled ***"Get It Together"***, and that while the song is playing you would like them to answer the questions on the **Journey Into Me** handout.
5. Distribute the **Journey Into Me** handout.
6. After the girls have answered the questions, share with them the remaining directives, and allow anyone who would like to an opportunity to share.
7. Always end the activity with the Five Star Girl Pledge.

Materials Needed:

1. **A Journey Into Me** handout
2. Trash can
3. Index Cards
4. Markers
5. Index Cards
6. Flip Chart
7. CD Player
8. India Arie's CD Voyage to India

A JOURNEY INTO ME

Before beginning the activity, write the following statement on the board. "*Sticks and Stones may break my bones, but words/names will never hurt me".* Ask each participants to explain what this means. Secondly, ask them if they believe this to be true. If so, why? If not, why not? Next, have them to write on a strip of paper, all the negative names they were called growing up. Make sure you do the same. It's always important for the facilitator to model the activity. Afterwards, ask if anyone would like to share. To encourage participation, the facilitator should go first. Remember, never coerce anyone to present. Have them to talk about how it made them feel and if the name still has some affect on them. Then, have those persons who shared, to ball up their paper and throw it in the trash. Even if you didn't share, encourage every girl to throw away their old baggage. Once everyone has completed the task, talk about the importance of throwing away old baggage in order to move forward. Just like when you check in at the airport, the first thing you check is your baggage.

Play the song, ***Get It Together***, written by India Arie. Be sure to listen to the music ahead of time to ensure that it is appropriate for your classroom and your comfort level. While the song is being played, have the student to answer the questions below:

1. Who were the 3 people that hurt India?
2. How was she hurt?
3. Out of the three people who hurt her, who do you think was the most damaging?
4. What do you think India kept inside?
5. Why do we hold painful memories inside?
6. What were the consequences of India not dealing with her pain?
7. What does India means when she says, *"...I've been redeemed from your anguish and pain."*
8. What assumptions can you conclude about India's childhood?
9. If any, how is your story similar or different to India's?

Module 11 Activity 1 Handout

ACTIVITY 2: BODY IMAGE/SELF IDENTITY

Activity Purpose:

The purpose of this activity is have girls to a look at society's perception of what a women should look and dress like in comparison to what they, as individuals, perceive of themselves.

Directions:

The girls will peruse magazines to look at as well as collect images of women – by society's standards, and then compare these images to what they feel about themselves.

Instructional Procedures:

1. Open with reciting the Five Star Girl Pledge.
2. Begin this activity by talking about how despite the advances made by the women's movement, young women are still being bombarded by exploitative images of women in the media. Talk about how with all of this to contend with, young women are often confused and conflicted about their self-image and perception.
3. Share with the girls that you have a pile of magazines that they are to go through and examine different images of women. As the girls examine the images they are to answer the questions on the **Body Image/Self Identity – Part I** handout.
4. Next the girls are to cut out the images, think about what the images are saying, and then answer the questions on the **Body Image/Self Identity – Part II** handout.
5. Once everyone has finished, allow those girls who would like to share an opportunity to do so.
6. Always end the activity with the Five Star Girl Pledge.

Materials Needed:

1. **Body Image/Self Identity - Part I** handout
2. **Body Image/Self Identity – Part II** handout
3. Magazines
4. Pens or pencils

Body Image / Sexual Identity – Part I

Despite the advances made by the women's movement, young women are still being bombarded by exploitative images of women in the media. With all of this to contend with, young women are often confused and conflicted about their self-image and perception. The movies and videos normally show women as sex crazed, submissive, materialistic divas. The activity below will give the participants an opportunity to reflect on how they view beauty.

Distribute these questions, prior to beginning the activity:

1. What actress or singer/hip-hop artist do you admire most today? What makes her attractive?
2. What makes a person attractive? Is it mainly based on appearance? [Points to bring up: humor, intelligence, kindness, wealth, patience, determination, compassion, being a good, student, employee, friend or neighbor]
3. What is considered today's ideal beauty? Does this ideal standard represent women from all different cultures?
4. Do most women or girls you know conform to this standard?
5. Who or what influences how you see yourself?
6. Have you ever tried to change your appearance to look like women on television or magazines?
7. Can we change parts of our bodies? Which ones and how? Have we really changed when we change these parts of our bodies? Are we better people? What parts of us can we not change? Does our inability to change some parts of our bodies mean we are unattractive? Why not?
8. What influences your personal style, self-image and sexual identity?
9. Have you ever tried to change your appearance to look like women on television or magazines?
10. Do women of color face different body image issues?
11. Is it difficult to discuss issues of sexual identity with your peers? Is there acceptance of alternative lifestyles within your community?

Module 11 Activity 2 Handout

BODY IMAGE / SEXUAL IDENTITY – PART II

During this activity girls will collect promoting images of beauty and attractiveness in major fashion and news magazines. Describe and list the physical characteristics in these ads (such as age, weight, race, etc.) and the lifestyles that are emphasized within them. In a journal or notebook track down and describe the number of daily ads in newspapers and television that reveal these images. As you do this activity, ask yourself questions like:

1. Do these ads reflect what real women look like?

2. Are these images harmful to women and girls' self-esteem?

3. Who do you think create these ads - men or women?

As you continue in this activity, now look for images of same sex preferences or bisexuality, ask yourself:

1. How are these images portrayed?

2. Is there a statement or prejudice that is being implied in the ad?

Finally, compare and contrast these images with the ones you collected in activity in the first part of the activity.

Module 11 Activity 2 Handout

MODULE TWELVE
BAGGAGE CHECK

Five Star Girl Quote:
"When you don't have a grip on life, it will definitely get a grip on you."
Jewel Diamond-Taylor

MODULE GOALS:

1. To encourage girls to take full responsibility for their destiny based upon how they live their lives.
2. To demonstrate how our choices dictate our outcome.

MODULE OVERVIEW:

When it's all said and done, we, not anyone else, have the final say about our lives. We control our decisions. We control our behavior. We control who we allow in our space. We determine high hard we want to work to reach our goals. We decide whether or not we want the trauma of our past to control our present. And we make these decisions consciously as well as unconsciously on a daily basis.

In a day where women are reaching heights in the corporate world that no one ever predicted they'd reach, we also have more women entering penal institutions for harsher crimes. Although we have research showing girls entering college at rates two times higher than that of their male counterparts, we also have research showing that girls are becoming more violent and harboring more angry which in turn causes them to make decisions that are rooted in their anger and not in their best interest. It is extremely important, therefore, for us to equip girls with strategies to deal with life's disappointments. It's imperative that we teach girls how to periodically take inventory of their personal space to assess the degree to which it may be cluttered with garbage that needs to be discarded, people who aren't productive, or ideals and beliefs that are self sabotaging.

Indeed it's a wonderful experience being female, yet the challenge rests with each individual to make the most of the experience. Too many women and/or girls are not fully enjoying themselves or their lives because they insist upon carrying around excess baggage i.e. pain, unforgiveness, unappreciative mates, non-fulfilling jobs, an inability to say no, uncertainty about their identity, and the list goes on. Now is the time...today is the day to concretely quality who you are and what you desire your life's course to be. It's all about ownership. Take responsibility for you!

MODULE ACTIVITIES:

1. Trash Can I Am Not
2. Circle of Certainty
3. Ladder of Success vs. Pile of Regrets

FACT FINDING:

- To serve young women effectively, programs must develop culturally-sensitive, gender-specific approaches. They must take into account the fact that girls' problems are often gender related (i.e., sexual abuse, male violence, role in the family, occupational inequality, early motherhood) and must develop gender-specific approaches. (Chesney-Lind & Shelden, 1998)

Activity 1: A Trash Can I Am Not

Activity Purpose:

The purpose of this activity is to have girls dispose of those things and/or people that really aren't serving a useful purpose in their lives.

Directions:

The girls will make a list of people and/or things that constantly dump on them, and make a decision to get those people or things out of their lives by physically and mentally discarding them.

Instructional Procedures:

1. Open with reciting the Five Star Girl Pledge.
2. Begin this activity by talking about how we make the mistake, particularly as women and girls, of thinking that we have to take more than we really do, and as a result we end up with a lot of excess baggage or unnecessary trash bombarding our personal space.
3. Share with the girls that for this activity they will be examining those things in their lives that make them feel trashy or useless as well as those people in their lives who continue to dump on them as if they are some kind of trash receptacle. After examining these things, the girls will make a conscious decision to discard what needs to be discarded in the trash receptable provided for them.
4. Distribute the **Trash Can I Am Not** handout.
5. Show the girls where the trash receptacle will be located.
6. After the girls have finished writing on their handout, allow those girls who would like to an opportunity to share.
7. Always end the activity with the Five Star Girl Pledge.

Materials Needed:

1. **A Trash Can I Am Not** handout
2. Trash can
3. Pens or pencils

I Trash Can I Am Not

Before beginning this activity, first take some time to identify those people in your life who continuously dump on you - without any regard for your feelings - as if you are their personal trash can. Secondly, identify those things in your life which represent *trash* and *filth*...things you know are no good for you. Thirdly, write the names of the people and a list of the things which are to be discarded on the handout provided. Finally, when directed to do so, you will place the people and the things in the trash can provided by the facilitator. Understand that physically placing these people and things in the trash receptacle is one thing, but mentally removing them from your mind and life is something you will have to continue to do as you remind yourself of this process.

People who dump on me disregardingly	Things I need to desperately disregard
________________	________________
________________	________________
________________	________________
________________	________________
________________	________________
________________	________________
________________	________________
________________	________________
________________	________________
________________	________________
________________	________________
________________	________________
________________	________________
________________	________________
________________	________________
________________	________________

Module 12 Activity 1 Handout

ACTIVITY 2: CIRCLE OF CERTAINTY

Activity Purpose:

The purpose of this activity is to teach girls how to put their lives, the people in their lives and the things in their lives in perspective.

Directions:

The girls will use the **Circle of Certainty** to assess and place things and people appropriately in their lives.

Instructional Procedures:

1. Open with reciting the Five Star Girl Pledge.
2. Begin this activity with a dialogue about boundaries and why its important for people and things to have an appropriately designated place in our lives. Talk about the danger of allowing people and things unsupervised access to places we may not want them to be in our existence.
3. Share with the girls that the **Circle of Certainty** handout is designed to give them a perspective about the three core levels of our existence, and that by using the circle we can get a better understanding of how to position people and things in our lives.
4. Distribute the **Circle of Certainty** handout and the corresponding handout.
5. After the girls have finished writing on their handout, allow those girls who would like to an opportunity to share.
6. Always end the activity with the Five Star Girl Pledge.

Materials Needed:

1. **A Circle of Certainty** handout
2. The corresponding Circle of Certainty handout
3. Pens or pencils

Circle of Certainty

As we maneuver through life one of the things we quickly discover is that there are very few guarantees. From one day to the next, things can change and change and change. If we are to life lives of balance and productivity, we must have a handle or a perspective about our lives; who's in our lives, what's in our lives and the level of importance these things have at it relates to our overall growth and development. The Circle of Certainty below illustrates the three core levels of our existence and what these cores represent. As you examine the circle, think about your life. Think about who and what goes where within the circle and on the separate handout begin to write those things in. Use this Circle of Certainty as a guide to help you keep your life in perspective as you move forward. Every now and then you may have to take some people and things off and/or add some people and things on—you decide.

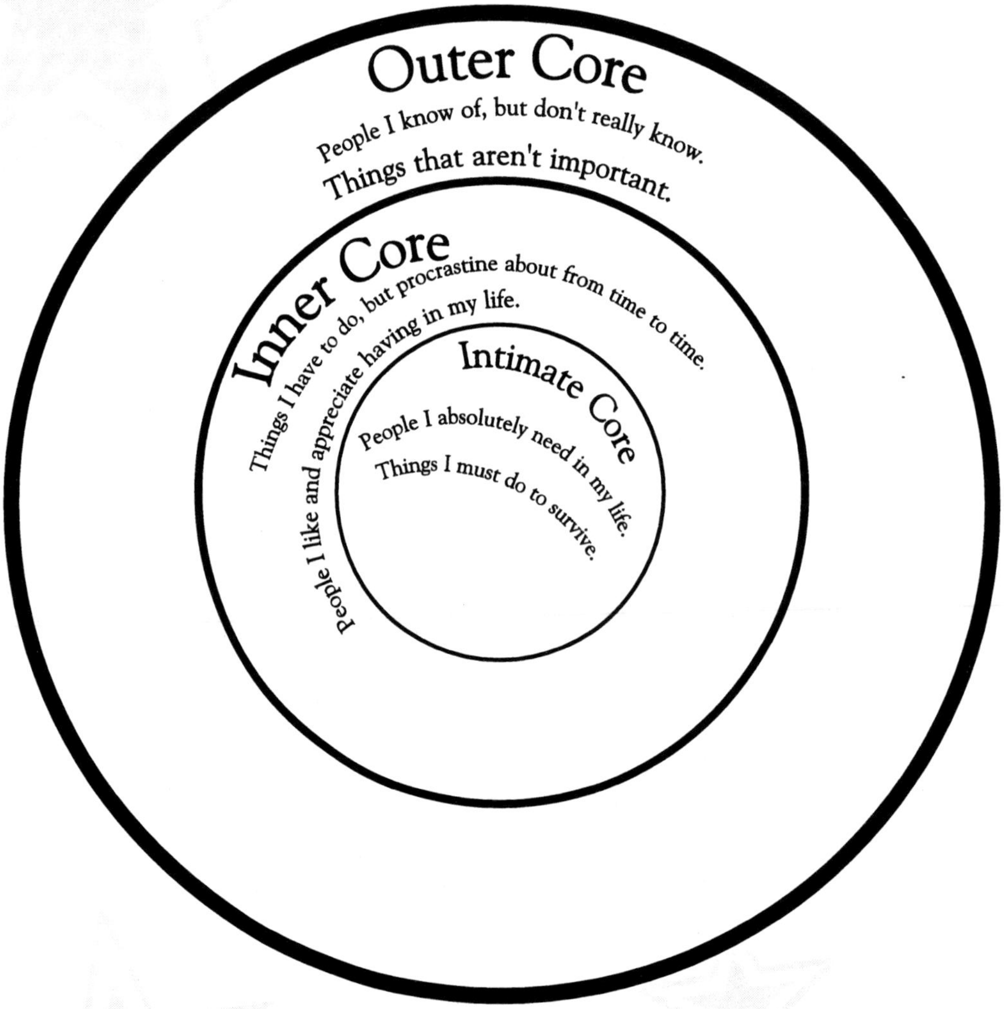

Module 12 Activity 2 Handout

CIRCLE OF CERTAINTY

Outer Core

People I know of, but don't really know. Things that aren't important.
Ex: A teacher who isn't a favorite. Whether or not I get a car at 16.

1. ______________________
2. ______________________
3. ______________________
4. ______________________
5. ______________________

Inner Core

People I like and appreciate having in my life. Things I have to do, but procrastinate about from time to time.
Ex: My girlfriend's mother. Homework, school assignments.

1. ______________________
2. ______________________
3. ______________________
4. ______________________
5. ______________________

Intimate Core

People I love and absolutely need in my life. Things I must do to survive.
Ex: My parents, my godmother. Learn, pray.

1. ______________________
2. ______________________
3. ______________________
4. ______________________
5. ______________________

Module 12 Activity 2 Handout

ACTIVITY 3: LADDER OF SUCCESS VS. PILES OF REGRETS

Activity Purpose:

The purpose of this activity is to demonstrate to girls how they, alone, have the capacity to determine the path that their life takes.

Directions:

The girls will first listen to the guest speaker (someone who started from the bottom and climbed their way to the top), ponder the things he/she shares, and then answer the questions on the **Success vs. Regrets** handout.

Instructional Procedures:

1. Open with reciting the Five Star Girl Pledge.
2. Begin this activity with a dialogue about *success,* and how we must have a determination for that which we want to achieve. Then talk about *regrets*, and how if we aren't careful our excuses will quickly and eventually accumulate to nothing more than a piles of regrets.
3. Share with the girls that you've invited a wonderful, successful guest in to speak to them about his/her success—the joys, the challenges, the obstacles, but most important their determination to succeed.
4. Introduce the guest speaker. If you can, get a bio ahead of time, make copies, and distribute a copy to each girl.
5. After the guest speaker has spoken, permit the girls to ask questions.
6. Following the questions and after the guest speaker has gone, distribute the **Success vs. Regrets** handout. Allow approximately 20 minutes for the girls to answer the questions.
7. After the girls have finished answering the questions, allow those girls who would like to an opportunity to share.
8. Before concluding the session pass out the **Ladder of Success vs. Pile of Regrets** handout.
9. Always end the activity with the Five Star Girl Pledge.

Materials Needed:

1. Guest speaker
2. **Success vs. Regrets** handout
3. **Ladder of Success vs. Piles of Regrets** handout
4. Pens or pencils

Success vs. Regrets

Whether we know it or not we are always establishing ourselves. Every day, with every decision, we are making a statement about our destination. Some of us choose to make every day count by doing something that puts us closer to our dream or our success. Others of us choose to mark time by taking for granted that tomorrow will be a better day than today to change. Unfortunately, for too many tomorrow – the day of change – never comes and they end up accumulating one pile after another of regrets when they very well could have been steadfastly climbing the ladder of success. By way of this activity you are asked to take a few moments to consider what you want your "todays" to be about. Read the questions and answer them only after you've taken a few minutes to honestly think about what it asks. Make sure that whatever you write is what you will purpose to do—at all cost. Your answers will be that which you hold yourself accountable to as you journey through.

1. How will I make the most of everyday?

2. What am I deliberately doing *now* to ensure that I am successful?

3. What is my plan to overcome obstacles?

4. How will I build or rebuild my strength when I get weak and discouraged?

5. What mechanisms do I have in place to ensure I stay on course?

6. What am I willing to do to be successful?

7. How will I keep distractions out of my way?

Module 12 Activity 3 Handout

THE LADDER OF SUCCESS VS. PILES OF REGRETS

There is a fine line between building success and building regrets. Our mind set and our language has to be such that it is complementary of what we want for ourselves. Therefore, be ever mindful of that which you think, because your success begins or ends in your mind. Read the statements on the ladder as well as the statements on the rock pile. See which statements you find yourself currently using the most, but ultimately make a commitment with yourself to only use those statements that will build success rather than regrets.

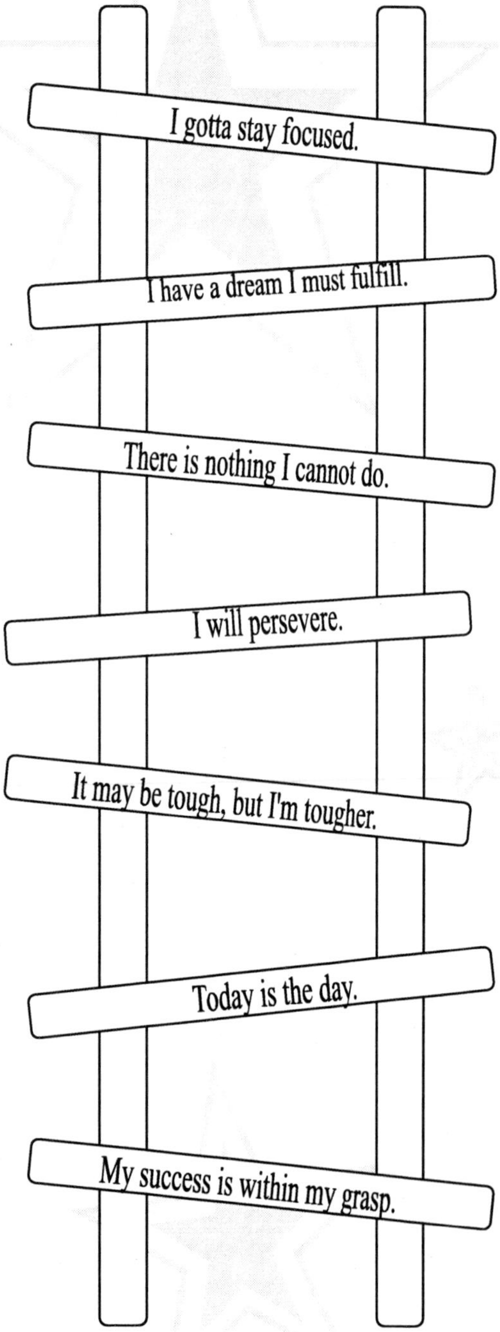

Module 12 Activity 3 Handout

SONG LYRICS FOR ACTIVITIES

"Outside" by Mariah Carey

Verse 1
It's hard to explain
Inherently just always been strange
Neither here nor there
Always somewhat out of place somewhere
Ambiguous
Without a sense of belonging to touch
Somewhere halfway
Feeling there's no one completely the same

Chorus 1
Standing alone
Eager to just
Believe it's good enough to be what
You really are
But in your heart
Uncertainty forever lies
And you'll always be
Somewhere on the
Outside

Verse 2
Early on, you face
The realization you don't
Have a space
Where you fit in
And recognize you
Where born to exist

Chorus 2
Standing alone
Eager to just
Believe it's good enough to be what
You really are
But in your heart
Uncertainty forever lies
And you'll always be
Somewhere on the
Outside

And it's hard
And it's hard
And it's hard

"Outside" by Mariah Carey continued

Bridge
Irreversibly
Falling in between
And it's hard
And it's hard
To be understood
As you are
As you are
Oh, and God knows
That you're standing on your own
Blind and unguided
Into a world divided
You're thrown
Where you're never quite the same
Although you try—try and try
To tell yourself
You really are
But in your heart—uncertainty forever lies
And you'll always be
Somewhere on the outside
You'll always be
Somewhere on the outside

"Treat Her Like A Lady" by Celine Dion

All the girl could want was a little attention
From a man who's strong and not to mention
Kiss and caressing her all night long
But all that boy wants is to hit and run off
He and his friends-they sit and they laugh
Going around talking 'bout the girls they used in the past

You're gonna get whats coming to you
For all the bad bad things you do to your

Lady, treat her like a lady
You'll make a good girl crazy
If you don't treat her like a lady
Lady, treat her like a lady
You'll make a good girl crazy
If you don't treat her like a lady

She stopped going to church, she don't wanna go to school
She left with anger when he took her for a fool
Even though her friends tell her to just keep cool
Didn't tell her from the start just what he had planned
Right in her face with another woman
Now she's in jail for attacking her man

You're gonna get whats coming to you
For all the bad bad things you do to your

Lady, treat her like a lady
You'll make a good girl crazy
If you don't treat her like a lady

Tell it to her straight, she can take the truth
Don't lead her on and leave her confused
Anyone would rather be alone than be used
Don't sit and think you'll hurt her feelings
She only wants to know just what the deal is
Next time beware of who's heart your breaking (or stealing)

You're gonna get whats coming to you
For all the bad bad things you do to your

Lady, treat her like a lady
You'll make a good girl crazy
If you don't treat her like a lady
Lady, treat her like a lady
You'll make a good girl crazy
If you don't treat her like a lady
Ooh!

"Get It Together" by India Arie

One shot to your heart without breaking your skin
No one has the power to hurt you like your kin
Kept it inside, didn't tell no one else
Didn't even wanna admit it to yourself
And now your chest burns and your back aches
From 15 years of holding the pain
And now you only have yourself to blame
If you continue to live this way

[Chorus:]
Get it together
You wanna heal your body
You have to heal your heart
Whatsoever you sow you will reap
Get it together

You can fly fly

Dark future ahead of me
That's what they say
I'd be starving if I ate all the lies they fed
Cause I've been redeemed from your anguish and pain
A miracle child I'm floating on a cloud
Cause the words that come from your mouth
You're the first to hear
Speak words of beauty and you will be there
No matter what anybody says
What matters most is what you think of yourself

[Chorus]

The choice is yours
No matter what it is
To choose life is to choose to forgive
You don't have to try
To hurt him and break his pride
To shake that weight off
And you will be ready to fly

One shot to your heart without breaking your skin
No one has the power to hurt you like your friends
Thought it will never change but this time moved on
An ugly duckling grew up to be a swan
And now your chest burns and your back aches
Because now the years are showing up on your face
But you're never be happy
And you'll never be whole
Until you see the beauty in growing old

"Never Give Up" by Yolanda Adams

Visions that can change the world trapped inside an ordinary girl
She looks just like me too afraid to dream out loud
And though it's simple your idea, it won't make sense to everybody
You need courage now If you're gonna persevere

To fulfill divine purpose, you gotta answer when you're called
So don't be afraid to face the world against all odds

[CHORUS]
Keep the dream alive don't let it die
If something deep inside keeps inspiring you to try, don't stop
And never give up, don't ever give up on you
Don't give up

Every victory comes in time, work today to change tomorrow
It gets easier, who's to say that you can't fly
Every step you take you get, closer to your destination
You can feel it now, don't you know you're almost there?

To fulfill divine purpose, you gotta answer when you're called
So don't be afraid to face the world against all odds

[CHORUS]
Keep the dream alive don't let it die
If something deep inside keeps inspiring you to try, don't stop
And never give up, don't ever give up on you

Sometimes life can place a stumbling block in your way
But you've gotta keep the faith, bring what's deep inside your heart to light
And never give up don't ever give up on you, Don't give up

[BRIDGE:]
Who holds the pieces to complete the puzzle?
The answer that can solve a mystery
The key that can unlock your understanding
It's all inside of you, you have everything you need yeahhhh

Sooooo, keep the dream alive don't let it die
If something deep inside, keeps inspiring you to try don't stop
And never give up, don't ever give up on you

Sometimes life can place a stumbling block in your way
But you're gotta keep the faith, bring what's deep inside your heart yeah your
Heart to the light
And never give up Don't ever give up on you

Nooo don't give up,
No, no, no, no don't give up
Oh, no, no, no, no don't...give...up

"Final Hour" by Lauryn Hill

I treat this like my thesis
well written topic
broken down into pieces.
I introduce then produce
words so profuse
it's abuse how I juice up this beat
like I'm deuce.
Two people both equal
like I'm Gemini
rather simeon
if I Jimmy on this lock I could pop it
You can't stop it
drop it
your whole crew's microscopic.
Like particles while I make international articles
and on the cover
don't discuss the baby mother business
I been in this third LP you can't tell me, I witness
first handed I'm candid
you can't stand it
respect demanded
and get flown around the planet.
Rock Hard like granite or steel
people feel Lauryn Hill from New-Ark to Israel
and this is real
so I keep makin' the street's ballads
while you lookin' for dressin' to go with your tossed salad.

You could get the money
you could get the power
but keep your eyes on the final hour

Now I be breakin' bread sippin Manichevitz wine
pay no mind party like it's 1999
but when it comes down to ground beef like Palestine
say your rhymes, let's see if that get you out your bend.
Now I'm a get the mozzarella like a Rockerfeller
still be in the church of Lalibela
singing hymns a cappella
whether posed in Maribella in Couture
or collectin' residuals from off the Score
I'm makin' sure
I'm with the 144
I've been here before this ain't a battle this is war.

"Final Hour" by Lauryn Hill continued

Word to Boonie
I makes a lot like a Sunni
get diplomatic immunity in every ghetto community
had opportunity went from
hoodshock to Hood-chic.
But it ain't what you cop
it's about what you keep
and even if there are leaks
you can't capsize this ship
cause I baptize my lips every time I take a sip.

You could get the money
you could get the power
but keep your eyes on the final hour

I'm about to change the focus
from the richest to the brokest
I wrote this opus
to reverse the hypnosis
whoever's closest
to the line's gonna win it
you gonna fall tryin to ball
while my team win the pennant
I'm about to be in it
for a minute
then run for senate
make a slum lord be the tenant
give his money to kids to spend it
and then amend it
every law that ever prevented
our survival since our arrival
documented in the bible
like Moses and Aaron
things gon change, it's apparent
and all the transparent gonna
be seen through
let God redeem you
keep your deen true
watch out what you cling to
you can get the green too
observe how a queen do
and I remain calm readin' the 73 Psalm
cause wit all this on I got the world in palm

You could get the money
you could get the power
but keep your eyes on the final hour

APPENDIX

The Appendix includes the paperwork for curriculum participants, parent involvement, and other helpful forms and information. The Project Director and/or designee should create a file for each participant.

The following documents should be included in the file:

Youth Consent Form

Youth Contract

Parent Contract

Parent-Youth Assessment (Home Visit)

Confidentiality Statement

Student Profile

Behavioral Incident Form

Behavioral Assessment Form

Community Service Report

Parent Support Letter

Praise Report

Youth Support Note

Helpful information about youth, abuse and neglect, and trauma:

Child Abuse and Neglect Advisory

Post-Traumatic Stress Disorder & Youth

SESSION CHECKLIST

Session # __________

The Session Checklist is designed to ensure that the facilitator is prepared for each session. Facilitators should develop a toolbox that includes the following materials so they are prepared for sessions. The checklist should be completed prior to each session.

- ✓ Flip Charts
- ✓ Construction paper/index cards
- ✓ Tape/glue
- ✓ Scissors
- ✓ String
- ✓ Stapler/staples
- ✓ Markers
- ✓ Pens/pencils
- ✓ Handouts ____
- ✓ Other supplies ____
- ✓ Reflection sheets

Facilitator's Notes:

____

____

____

____

____

____

SESSION ATTENDANCE SHEET

Session No.: ____________________ Date: ______________________________

Facilitator(s): ____

Attendees:

1. ____________________ 14. ____________________
2. ____________________ 15. ____________________
3. ____________________ 16. ____________________
4. ____________________ 17. ____________________
5. ____________________ 18. ____________________
6. ____________________ 19. ____________________
7. ____________________ 20. ____________________
8. ____________________ 21. ____________________
9. ____________________ 22. ____________________
10. ____________________ 23. ____________________
11. ____________________ 24. ____________________
12. ____________________ 25. ____________________
13. ____________________ 26. ____________________

Absentee List (include names of youth who are not in attendance):

1. ____________________ 5. ____________________
2. ____________________ 6. ____________________
3. ____________________ 7. ____________________
4. ____________________ 8. ____________________

YOUTH CONSENT FORM

Dare to Be Queen: A Wholistic & Comprehensive Curriculum for Girls

PROJECT DIRECTOR: ____

PARTICIPANT'S NAME: ____

PURPOSE/DESCRIPTION
The purpose of the project is to empower girls and equip them with the necessary tools to make healthy, responsible decisions. The project will also heighten girls' awareness about the potential distractions of our society.

PROCEDURE/TASK
If you allow your child to participate in this project, she will participate beginning ____________ and ending ____________. The project will entail your daughter taking part in a variety of educationally enhancing, culturally enriching, mentally stimulating activities.

CONFIDENTIALITY
All information will be kept confidential. Program participants sign an agreement to keep any personal information discussed during the sessions confidential.

PROJECT STATEMENT
The project goal is to reduce the likelihood that girls will participate in self-sabotaging behaviors. Using a variety of techniques, girls will explore healthy and innovative alternatives to trouble, delinquency, and irresponsible decisions.

SUBJECT STATEMENT
I have received a copy of this consent form. I fully understand the purpose of the project and I give my child permission to participate. Additionally, photographs taken during the project may be used for news stories and/or future publications.

______________________________________ ______________
Signature of Parent/Guardian Date

______________________________________ ______________
Signature of Participant Date

______________________________________ ______________
Signature of Project Director Date

YOUTH CONTRACT

Dare to Be Queen: A Wholistic & Comprehensive Curriculum for Girls

This is an agreement between ______________________________ and ___________________________.
Youth (print) Facilitator (print)

Per the terms of this contract, the youth agree to:

- ✓ Complete all phases of the workbook
- ✓ Participate in the *Dare to Be Queen* Weekend Retreat
- ✓ Listen to and respect the adults and youth involved in *Dare to Be Queen*
- ✓ Understand the cycle of deception and manipulation within our society and develop the skills to avoid being a victim and/or a perpetrator
- ✓ Learn to appreciate the importance of life and working with other girls

______________________________ ________________
Youth Signature Date

______________________________ ________________
Signature of Parent/Guardian Date

______________________________ ________________
Signature of Facilitator Date

PARENT CONTRACT

Dare to Be Queen: A Wholistic & Comprehensive Curriculum for Girls

Parent Involvement is a crucial component to the success of the Dare to Be Queen (DTBQ) instrument. In an effort to promote and ensure greater parental participation, the DTBQ planning team and the facilitator will schedule four (4) "parent support" gatherings.

This is an agreement between ______________________________ and ______________________________.
Parent/Guardian (print) Facilitator (print)

Parents will be notified of the date for the parent support gatherings. The following are additional requirements of parents who have girls enrolled in the DTBQ process.

- ✓ Participate in DTBQ parent support gatherings
- ✓ Communicate with DTBQ staff regarding matters involving their daughter
- ✓ Participate in the DTBQ Karamu (final ceremony)
- ✓ Participate in 6 month follow up after project is over

____ ____________
Parent/Guardian Signature Date

____ ____________
Signature of Facilitator Date

PARENT-YOUTH ASSESSMENT (HOME VISIT)

Dare to Be Queen: A Wholistic & Comprehensive Curriculum for Girls

Youth Name ____________________ Date ________________

Parent/Guardian(s) ____________________ School/Agency______________

Address __________________________ Zip Code ______________

Please indicate concerns that the parent/guardian(s) have about their daughter. These concerns may include home, school, and community. The facilitator should encourage the parent to identify specific behaviors of concern.

Questions:

How is your child doing in school? Are there any learning or conduct issues?

Is your child involved in positive activities (e.g., helping at home, after-school activities?

Is your child involved in negative activities (e.g., substance use, hanging in the streets)?

What would you like for your child to get out of participating in Dare to Be Queen?

Identified Concerns	Additional Comments

CONFIDENTIALITY STATEMENT

Dare To Be Queen: A Wholistic & Comprehensive Curriculum for Girls was created to help young girls begin to address the growing issues related to our society's deceptive and demeaning portrayal of girls. Too often, girls in our communities are faced with trying to go along to get along, and in the process end up compromising their values and standards.

Several of the sessions contained in the workbook require youth to share sensitive information about themselves, family and friends. It is important that participants agree to keep any information discussed within the group. Any names, individual incidents, and situations that may have occurred at home, during school, or in the community will be held in the strictest confidence.

I have read and understand the above Confidentiality Statement and agree to keep all information discussed, by me and others, during the sessions confidential.

______________________________________ ____________________
Youth Signature Date

______________________________________ ____________________
Signature of Parent/Guardian Date

______________________________________ ____________________
Signature of Facilitator Date

STUDENT PROFILE

Date Enrolled: ______________________ Date of Birth: ______________________

Name: ______________________ Telephone #: ______________________

Address: ______________________ City/State/Zip code: ______________________

Parent/Guardian(s): ______________________

SHORT TERM GOALS: ______________________

____

____

LONG TERM GOALS: ______________________

____

____

ACADEMIC PROGRESS

School: ______________________ Grade: ________ Teacher: ______________

	1st Quarter	2nd Quarter	3rd Quarter	4th Quarter
English	________	________	________	________
Math	________	________	________	________
Science	________	________	________	________
Social Stud.	________	________	________	________
Other	________	________	________	________

** The facilitator will be responsible for documenting student performance based on school records. The facilitator will do follow up with the student up to three months after the intervention has been completed.

BEHAVIORAL INCIDENT FORM

Girl's Name:________________________________ Facilitator:___________________________

Check Appropriate Box:

☐ Fighting ☐ Disrespectful to others ☐ Not completing assignments

☐ Outburst ☐ Repeated Absences ☐ Referral for additional services

Date Description of Incident

________ ____

________ ____

________ ____

________ ____

________ ____

________ ____

Actions Taken By Staff:

____

____

____

____

____

BEHAVIORAL ASSESSMENT FORM

Student's Name:____

Coding System

A. Physical aggression is defined as action directed toward another person (to attack and/or lash out toward another individual): hitting, pushing, shoving, kicking, biting, spitting, throwing objects (books and/or other things)

B. Verbal aggression, intimidation, and/or disrespect toward others: profanity, threats of physical violence, and/or behavior described as disrespectful or disruptive

C. Violations which requires police intervention: possession of weapons or narcotics, physical assault where a student or school personnel seek criminal charges

Date	Code	Description of Incident

** Copies of the Behavioral Assessment Form should be kept in the student's file and one copy should be mailed to the parent/guardian.

COMMUNITY SERVICE REPORT

Name: ____ Program Year: __________

Check (□) One

__ Nursing home visit/activity
__ Feeding the homeless
__ Volunteer at community event
__ Tutoring younger students
__ Community Clean up
__ Other

AUTHORIZED SIGNATURE	DATE
____________________________________	_____________
____________________________________	_____________
____________________________________	_____________
____________________________________	_____________
____________________________________	_____________
____________________________________	_____________
____________________________________	_____________
____________________________________	_____________
____________________________________	_____________
____________________________________	_____________
____________________________________	_____________
____________________________________	_____________

PARENT SUPPORT LETTER

Date:

Dear Parent:

We would like to thank you for allowing us to meet with your family to discuss enrolling________________________________ in Dare to Be Queen (DTBQ). The home visit is an important part of the DTBQ process as it allows us to meet with parents in an effort to solicit your full participation as your child embarks upon a journey toward womanhood.

As I am sure you are aware, our female children are being deceived and manipulated by our society's overwhelming misrepresentation of what our daughters should look like and dress like. To this end, DTBQ represents an opportunity for young girls to explore womanhood as they deal with the many complex facets of being a young girl and becoming a women.

DTBQ was developed to support, assist and be used as a resource for parents to improve the quality of life for their daughters. The instrument is designed to educate, equip and empower mentally, socially, spiritually, educationally and physically.

We are looking forward to a powerful, productive and safe year teaching, coaching, and modeling appropriate behaviors for young girls.

Once again, thank you for your support in our effort to create "Five Star Girls."

____

Facilitator(s)

Every girl in the world needs an adult
to be completely sold out about their potential.
Mischa Green

PRAISE REPORT

The Praise Report is recommended to be used by the facilitator as a way to acknowledge the accomplishment of the girls' involvement in Dare to Be Queen (DTBQ). Often, the parents of young people only receive feedback from teachers, counselors, coaches and advocates when a problem arises. The Praise report is a proactive instrument which will be sent home to the parent to acknowledge strides in behavior, attitude and willingness to participate.

☐ Cut out and make copies

Praise Report

Dare To Be Queen

Name: ____

Program Location: ______________________ Date: ____________

Facilitator's Name: ______________________________________

Comments: ____

____

____

YOUTH SUPPORT NOTE

The Youth Support Message is recommended to be used by the facilitator as a way to make parents/guardians aware of disciplinary issues. The Youth Support Message is designed to encourage a solid relationship between the parent, youth and DTBQ staff. The Youth Support Message will be sent home to the parent/guardian. The facilitator may indicate the need for a parent meeting.

☐ Cut out and make copies

YOUTH SUPPORT NOTE

Name: ______________________________

Program Location: ______________ Date: __________

Facilitator's Name: ______________

Behavior:

____

____

Comments:

____

____

EMERGENCY PHONE NUMBERS

This workbook deals with serious issues that effect youth. As such, it is important that you have resources if participating youth need assistance or guidance. Below are emergency phone numbers as well as a Child Abuse and Neglect Advisory that talks about your responsibilities as a person working with youth. Please keep in mind that this information is included as a precaution, not as an indicator that you will need to deal with these issues.

Crisis hotlines usually provide short-term crisis intervention and counseling and referrals to local community resources. They may counsel on parent-child conflicts, marital and family issues, suicide, pregnancy, runaway youth, physical and sexual abuse, drug abuse, domestic violence, and other issues.

All hotlines operate 24 hours a day, seven days a week.

Emergency/Crisis	
Boys Town Suicide and Crisis Line	1- 800-448-3000
Covenant House Hotline	1- 800-999-9999
National Youth Crisis Hotline	1-800-442-HOPE (4673)
Suicide Hotline	1-800-333-4313
Alcohol and Drug Abuse	
Drug Hotline	1-800-333-4313
National Drug Information Treatment and Referral Hotline	1-800-662-HELP (4357)
Crisis Counseling and Services for Runaways	
National Runaway Switchboard	1-800-621-4000
Child Abuse, Sexual Assault/Rape and Domestic Violence	
Childhelp USA	1-800-422-4453
National Child Abuse Hotline	1-800-25-ABUSE (22873)
National Domestic Violence Hotline	1-800-799-SAFE (7233)
RAINN National Rape Crisis Hotline	1-800-656-HOPE (4673)

** Consult your local jurisdictions for information and referrals.

CHILD ABUSE AND NEGLECT ADVISORY

Know your responsibility.

Child abuse, neglect and abandonment are serious issues which require the involvement of all private citizens and **professionals** who work with youth and families. In most states, strict reporting guidelines require that anyone who suspects that a child has been, or is being, mistreated report the matter to local law enforcement and/or the Department of Social Services or Child Protective Services.

Any professional who knowingly fails to make a required report of child abuse may be subject to certain professional sanctions. These sanctions may include loss of professional licensor, certification and the possibility of civil and/or criminal prosecution. Any individual who in good faith makes a report of abuse or neglect is ***immune*** from civil or criminal penalty. This information is designed to protect citizens and individuals who work with youth and families. Child abuse and neglect are serious matters!

The following information is provided so that you will be familiar with the physical and behavioral indicators of child abuse and neglect. Please note that the presence of any of these indicators does not necessarily mean a child is being abused or neglected. They may lead you to suspect abuse or neglect and therefore, to report it.

INDICATORS OF POSSIBLE PHYSICAL ABUSE

Physical Indicators
Bruises, on any infant, facial bruises; in unusual places; in patterns; in clusters; various stages of healing.

Burns; caused by immersion in hot liquid, cigarettes burns usually on palms of hands; burns associated with hot implements, curling irons or caused by ropes that indicate confinement. Welts, cuts, abrasions, fractures, and other internal injuries. Since these injuries may occur through normal childhood experiences, they should only cause concern when coupled with some other physical or behavioral indicators. You should only be concerned if the injury does not seem likely to have resulted from normal activity, given the age and physical development.

Behavioral Indicators
Child: overly compliant, shy or aggressive behavior; avoids parents; inhibited crying; hyperactive, avoids physical contact; low tolerance for frustration; distrustful; inappropriate sexual speech or behavior

Parent: holds unrealistic expectations for the child's physical or emotional development; low sense of self-esteem; sees the child as "bad or evil"; inappropriate coping skills.

POST TRAUMATIC STRESS DISORDER (PTSD) & YOUTH

Post-Traumatic Stress Disorder is an anxiety disorder that can develop after exposure to frightening events. Traumatic events that can trigger PTSD include murders, violent assaults, rapes and natural disasters.

Q: What are the symptoms of PTSD?
A: Youth may re-experience the trauma through nightmares. Other symptoms include trouble falling asleep, irritability or outbursts, feelings of vulnerability, and difficulty concentrating or remembering.

Q: How common is PTSD?
A: It is estimated that 40% of Americans have witnessed at least one major trauma. Other reports estimate that urban youth are more likely to be exposed to numerous traumatic events by the age of 12 due to the rates of homicide in urban communities.

Q: What are the implications of PTSD for urban African American males?
A: Due to the alarming rates of violence in urban communities, mental health professionals have seen an increase in incidents of PTSD. Additionally, mental health professionals site suicide, depression, feelings of hopelessness and death anxiety. (Suicide among African American males experienced the highest increase among any other group between the ages of 15-19 according to the Centers for Disease Control.)

Q: What kinds of traumatic events can cause PTSD?
A: PTSD can result from any severe stressor or catastrophic event. These events may include: Rape/sexual assault, beating, stabbing, witnessing a homicide, torture, animal attacks (pit bull attacks) riots, bombing or natural disaster (hurricane, flood, earthquake).

Q: What are the potential effects of PTSD?
A: If untreated, PTSD can cause serious impact to an individual's self concept and mental health status. Specific issues related to: depression, suicide, violence, guilt, social isolation, family disruption, low self-esteem, sexual dysfunction, drug addictions, and impaired relationships.

Q: What treatments are recommended for children and youth experiencing PTSD?
A: One of the most effective treatments for PTSD is a survivors group. A survivors group is a group of 5 to 10 individuals that meet weekly to discuss feelings and help each other address challenges. The group should be run or advised by a trained mental health professional.

For more information about PTSD, consult with a local mental health provider or review the list of national resources in the Resource Guide.

Reactions to Trauma
Typically, nightmares and flashbacks are the two most common reactions to witnessing a traumatic event. The following are list of additional physical and emotional reactions.

Physical Reactions:
aches and pains like headaches, backaches or stomachaches
changes in sleep patterns
constipation or diarrhea
easily startled by noises or unexpected touch

Emotional Reactions:
adopts fatalistic world view (the world is coming to an end)
shock or disbelief
grief
disorientation
hyper-alertness or hyper-vigilance
denial
irritability and/or restlessness
intrusive/unwanted/unexpected thoughts of the traumatic event
outburst and anger
concerns over burdening others with problems
feelings of helplessness
feelings of panic or feelings
tendency to isolate oneself
emotional numbing
difficulty trusting
difficulty concentrating or remembering
feelings of self-blame or survivor guilt
increase use of alcohol or drugs

Source: Post-Traumatic Stress Disorder: A Guide to Healing, Recovery and Growth by Glen Schiraldi, Ph.D. and *Violence Among Inner City High School Students and Post Traumatic Stress Disorder* by Esther Jenkins, Ph.D. and Carl Bell, Ph.D. in Anxiety Disorders in African Americans edited by Steven Friedman.

SUGGESTED WEBSITES

www.academic.org Expect the Best from a Girl. That's What you'll get. This site is developed at Mount Holyoke College to explore differences in EXPERIENCE and expectation that account for many of the differences in choices and PERFORMANCE.

www.agirlsworld.com A Girl's World Online Clubhouse was launched in June of 1996, and has among several goals: To encourage and empower 7-17 year old girls to become active contributors, not passive consumers of media and the Internet.

www.girlgeeks.org Girl Geeks is a site that continues to encourage women to develop their careers in technology among other things.

www.kembasmithfoundation.org A website for girls to become familiar with the life and purpose of Kemba Smith, her crusade to challenge and change laws, as well as her commitment to provide mentors for young girls who are in need of direction.

www.womeninworldhistory.com Women in World History Curriculum is an interactive site full of information and resources about women's experiences in world history. For teachers, teenagers, parents, and history buffs.

www.teenvoices.com Teen Voices Online is the original magazine written by, for, and about teenagers.

www.womenssportspage.com Women's Sports Page is one of the largest collections of links to sites on women in sports.

www.newmoon.org New Moon Magazine by contrast, challenges stereotypes by accepting girls as they are, listening to them, and honoring their diverse experience and dreams.

www.blackgirlmagazine.com As the first magazine of its kind, Black Girl Magazine focuses on promoting positive messages and imagery among African American teens, while offering insightful coverage of history, culture, lifestyle, and entertainment news from a unique perspective.

www.teenwire.com Teen Wire is the leading Web site for teens needing information about sexual health.

www.girlsinc.org Girls Incorporated is a national youth organization dedicated to helping every girl become strong, smart and bold

www.cybergrrl.com Cybergrrl is a useful, comic, and very practical listing of information on issues of concern to girls. Includes a search engine.

www.uah.edu/colleges/liberal/womensstudies/girls.html is a search engine for other girls "only" websites

SUGGESTED READINGS

Angelou, Maya. *Phenomenal Woman.* (Random House, Inc. 1994).

Banks, Tyra. *Tyra's Beauty: Inside & Out.* (HarperCollins, 1998).

Bingham, Mindy, Edmondson, Judy and Stryker, Sandy. *Choices: A Teen Women's Journal for Self Awareness and Personal Planning.* (Advocacy Press, 1984-Updated 1993).

Carlip, Hilary. *Girl Power: Young Women Speak Out!* (Warner Books, 1995).

Covey, Sean. *The 7 Habits of Highly Effective Teens: The Ultimate Teenage Success Guide.* (Fireside, 1998).

Ferebee, Janice. *Got It Goin' On: An Image Awareness Guide for Young Ladies.* (Janice Ferebee, 1996).

Green, Mischa. *Sacred: 100 Affirmations for Girls.* (Morals and Values Press, 2004).

Hansberry, Lorraine. *To Be Young, Gifted and Black.* (Random House, 1998).

Hurston, Zora Neale. *Their Eyes Were Watching God.* (HarperCollins, 1998).

Johnston, Andrea. *Girls Speak Out: Finding Your True Self.* (Scholastic Press, 1997).

Mack, Cassandra. *Cool, Confident & Strong: 52 Moves for Girls.* (Cassandra Mack, 2005).

Morrison, Toni. *Sula.* (Random House, 1991).

Simmons, Rachel. *Odd Girl Out.* (Harcourt Books, 2002).

Souljah, Sister. *No Disrespect.* (First Vintage Books, 1996).

Taylor, Susan. *In the Spirit.* (HarperCollins, 1993).

Vanzant, Iyanla. *Acts of Faith: Daily Affirmations for People of Color.* (Simon & Schuster, Inc. 1993.

Vanzant, Iyanla. *Don't Give It Away: A Book of Self-Awareness and Self-Affirmations for Young Women.* (Simon & Schuster, Inc. 1999).

Wiseman, Rosalind. *Queenbees & Wannabes: Helping Your Daughter Survive Cliques, Gossip, Boyfriends & Other Realities of Adolescence.* (Three Rivers Press, 2002.)

ORDERING INFORMATION

Name: ____

Agency/School: ____

Address: ____

City, State: ______________________________ Zip Code: ____________

Number of Copies: _____ + $3.00 S&H = $_____

Send check/money order for $35.00, plus $3.00 shipping & handling **per curriculum** to:

Urban Leadership Institute
2437 Maryland Avenue
Baltimore, Maryland 21218

You may also order copies of the curriculum as well as other publications by the authors on our website: www.urbanyouth.org.

241108-5-100-60W